学ぶ人は、
変えて
ゆく人だ。

目の前にある問題はもちろん、

人生の問いや、

社会の課題を自ら見つけ、

挑み続けるために、人は学ぶ。

「学び」で、

少しずつ世界は変えてゆける。

いつでも、どこでも、誰でも、

学ぶことができる世の中へ。

旺文社

2024年度版

文部科学省後援

英検®

準2級

過去6回
全問題集

旺文社

この問題カードは切り取って，本番の面接の練習用にしてください。
質問は p.45 にありますので，参考にしてください。

Studying Abroad Online

Today, many people study abroad. However, it sometimes takes a lot of time and money to go to other countries. Now, technology is playing an important role. Some people take online classes that are held by foreign schools, and by doing so they can experience studying abroad without leaving their own countries.

A

B

問題カード

この問題カードは切り取って，本番の面接の練習用にしてください。
質問は p.47 にありますので，参考にしてください。

Online Discount Stores

Today, discount stores on the Internet are attracting attention. People can buy things at lower prices, and as a result they find online discount stores helpful. However, people in some areas can have trouble using them. For example, they need to wait a long time for products to be delivered.

A

B

この問題カードは切り取って，本番の面接の練習用にしてください。
質問は p.69 にありますので，参考にしてください。

Outdoor Activities

Outdoor activities are popular with people of all ages. For example, camping in nature is fun, and many people enjoy cooking outdoors. However, some people do not pay enough attention to others around them, and as a result they cause problems for other campers. People should think about others when enjoying outdoor activities.

A

B

問題カード

この問題カードは切り取って，本番の面接の練習用にしてください。
質問は p.71 にありますので，参考にしてください。

Better Beaches

Today, beaches are popular with people of all ages. However, keeping beaches in good condition is hard work. Now, technology is playing an important role. Some towns use robots that clean beaches, and in this way they try to make the environment of their beaches better. Such robots are becoming more common.

A

B

この問題カードは切り取って，本番の面接の練習用にしてください。
質問は p.93 にありますので，参考にしてください。

Keeping the Air Clean

Today, air cleaners play important roles in places such as hospitals and schools. However, air cleaners can be very big and difficult to put in every room. Now, some companies are making smaller types of air cleaners, and by doing so they help more places to keep the air clean.

A

B

この問題カードは切り取って，本番の面接の練習用にしてください。
質問は p.95 にありますので，参考にしてください。

Staying Open All Night

In Japan, there are many stores that are open all day and night. However, some stores worry about the cost of staying open 24 hours, so they choose to close at night. Some customers do not think this is convenient, but more stores will probably stop staying open all night.

A

B

2023年度第2回　英検準2級　解答用紙

解答欄

問題番号		1	2	3	4
1	(1)	①	②	③	④
	(2)	①	②	③	④
	(3)	①	②	③	④
	(4)	①	②	③	④
	(5)	①	②	③	④
	(6)	①	②	③	④
	(7)	①	②	③	④
	(8)	①	②	③	④
	(9)	①	②	③	④
	(10)	①	②	③	④
	(11)	①	②	③	④
	(12)	①	②	③	④
	(13)	①	②	③	④
	(14)	①	②	③	④
	(15)	①	②	③	④
	(16)	①	②	③	④
	(17)	①	②	③	④
	(18)	①	②	③	④
	(19)	①	②	③	④
	(20)	①	②	③	④

解答欄

問題番号		1	2	3	4
2	(21)	①	②	③	④
	(22)	①	②	③	④
	(23)	①	②	③	④
	(24)	①	②	③	④
	(25)	①	②	③	④
3	(26)	①	②	③	④
	(27)	①	②	③	④
	(28)	①	②	③	④
	(29)	①	②	③	④
	(30)	①	②	③	④
4	(31)	①	②	③	④
	(32)	①	②	③	④
	(33)	①	②	③	④
	(34)	①	②	③	④
	(35)	①	②	③	④
	(36)	①	②	③	④
	(37)	①	②	③	④

※筆記5の解答欄はこの裏にあります。

リスニング解答欄

問題番号		1	2	3	4
	例題	①	②	●	
第1部	No.1	①	②	③	
	No.2	①	②	③	
	No.3	①	②	③	
	No.4	①	②	③	
	No.5	①	②	③	
	No.6	①	②	③	
	No.7	①	②	③	
	No.8	①	②	③	
	No.9	①	②	③	
	No.10	①	②	③	
第2部	No.11	①	②	③	④
	No.12	①	②	③	④
	No.13	①	②	③	④
	No.14	①	②	③	④
	No.15	①	②	③	④
	No.16	①	②	③	④
	No.17	①	②	③	④
	No.18	①	②	③	④
	No.19	①	②	③	④
	No.20	①	②	③	④
第3部	No.21	①	②	③	④
	No.22	①	②	③	④
	No.23	①	②	③	④
	No.24	①	②	③	④
	No.25	①	②	③	④
	No.26	①	②	③	④
	No.27	①	②	③	④
	No.28	①	②	③	④
	No.29	①	②	③	④
	No.30	①	②	③	④

※実際の解答用紙に似せていますが，デザイン・サイズは異なります。

切り取り線

●記入上の注意（記述形式）
・指示事項を守り，文字は，はっきりと分かりやすく書いてください。
・太枠に囲まれた部分のみが採点の対象です。

5 ライティング解答欄

5

10

15

2023年度第1回　英検準2級　解答用紙

解答欄

問題番号	1	2	3	4
(1)	①	②	③	④
(2)	①	②	③	④
(3)	①	②	③	④
(4)	①	②	③	④
(5)	①	②	③	④
(6)	①	②	③	④
(7)	①	②	③	④
(8)	①	②	③	④
(9)	①	②	③	④
(10)	①	②	③	④
(11)	①	②	③	④
(12)	①	②	③	④
(13)	①	②	③	④
(14)	①	②	③	④
(15)	①	②	③	④
(16)	①	②	③	④
(17)	①	②	③	④
(18)	①	②	③	④
(19)	①	②	③	④
(20)	①	②	③	④

（問題番号1）

解答欄

問題番号	1	2	3	4
(21)	①	②	③	④
(22)	①	②	③	④
(23)	①	②	③	④
(24)	①	②	③	④
(25)	①	②	③	④
(26)	①	②	③	④
(27)	①	②	③	④
(28)	①	②	③	④
(29)	①	②	③	④
(30)	①	②	③	④
(31)	①	②	③	④
(32)	①	②	③	④
(33)	①	②	③	④
(34)	①	②	③	④
(35)	①	②	③	④
(36)	①	②	③	④
(37)	①	②	③	④

（問題番号 2：(21)-(25)、3：(26)-(30)、4：(31)-(37)）

※筆記5の解答欄はこの裏にあります。

リスニング解答欄

問題番号	1	2	3	4
例題	①	②	●	
No.1	①	②	③	
No.2	①	②	③	
No.3	①	②	③	
No.4	①	②	③	
No.5	①	②	③	
No.6	①	②	③	
No.7	①	②	③	
No.8	①	②	③	
No.9	①	②	③	
No.10	①	②	③	
No.11	①	②	③	④
No.12	①	②	③	④
No.13	①	②	③	④
No.14	①	②	③	④
No.15	①	②	③	④
No.16	①	②	③	④
No.17	①	②	③	④
No.18	①	②	③	④
No.19	①	②	③	④
No.20	①	②	③	④
No.21	①	②	③	④
No.22	①	②	③	④
No.23	①	②	③	④
No.24	①	②	③	④
No.25	①	②	③	④
No.26	①	②	③	④
No.27	①	②	③	④
No.28	①	②	③	④
No.29	①	②	③	④
No.30	①	②	③	④

（例題-No.10：第1部、No.11-No.20：第2部、No.21-No.30：第3部）

※実際の解答用紙に似せていますが，デザイン・サイズは異なります。

切り取り線

●記入上の注意（記述形式）
・指示事項を守り，文字は，はっきりと分かりやすく書いてください。
・太枠に囲まれた部分のみが採点の対象です。

5 ライティング解答欄

| |
| |
| |
| |
| |
| 5 |
| |
| |
| |
| |
| 10 |
| |
| |
| |
| |
| 15 |

2022年度第3回　英検準2級　解答用紙

【注意事項】

① 解答にはHBの黒鉛筆（シャープペンシルも可）を使用し，解答を訂正する場合には消しゴムで完全に消してください。

② 解答用紙は絶対に汚したり折り曲げたり，所定以外のところへの記入はしないでください。

③ マーク例

良い例	悪い例
●	◐ ✖ ◓

これ以下の濃さのマークは読めません。

解　答　欄

問題番号	1	2	3	4
(1)	①	②	③	④
(2)	①	②	③	④
(3)	①	②	③	④
(4)	①	②	③	④
(5)	①	②	③	④
(6)	①	②	③	④
(7)	①	②	③	④
(8)	①	②	③	④
(9)	①	②	③	④
(10)	①	②	③	④
(11)	①	②	③	④
(12)	①	②	③	④
(13)	①	②	③	④
(14)	①	②	③	④
(15)	①	②	③	④
(16)	①	②	③	④
(17)	①	②	③	④
(18)	①	②	③	④
(19)	①	②	③	④
(20)	①	②	③	④

（左欄は**1**）

解　答　欄

問題番号	1	2	3	4
(21)	①	②	③	④
(22)	①	②	③	④
(23)	①	②	③	④
(24)	①	②	③	④
(25)	①	②	③	④
(26)	①	②	③	④
(27)	①	②	③	④
(28)	①	②	③	④
(29)	①	②	③	④
(30)	①	②	③	④
(31)	①	②	③	④
(32)	①	②	③	④
(33)	①	②	③	④
(34)	①	②	③	④
(35)	①	②	③	④
(36)	①	②	③	④
(37)	①	②	③	④

（(21)～(25)は**2**，(26)～(30)は**3**，(31)～(37)は**4**）

※筆記5の解答欄はこの裏にあります。

リスニング解答欄

問題番号	1	2	3	4
例題	①	②	●	
No.1	①	②	③	
No.2	①	②	③	
No.3	①	②	③	
No.4	①	②	③	
No.5	①	②	③	
No.6	①	②	③	
No.7	①	②	③	
No.8	①	②	③	
No.9	①	②	③	
No.10	①	②	③	
No.11	①	②	③	④
No.12	①	②	③	④
No.13	①	②	③	④
No.14	①	②	③	④
No.15	①	②	③	④
No.16	①	②	③	④
No.17	①	②	③	④
No.18	①	②	③	④
No.19	①	②	③	④
No.20	①	②	③	④
No.21	①	②	③	④
No.22	①	②	③	④
No.23	①	②	③	④
No.24	①	②	③	④
No.25	①	②	③	④
No.26	①	②	③	④
No.27	①	②	③	④
No.28	①	②	③	④
No.29	①	②	③	④
No.30	①	②	③	④

（No.1～No.10は**第1部**，No.11～No.20は**第2部**，No.21～No.30は**第3部**）

※実際の解答用紙に似せていますが，デザイン・サイズは異なります。

5 ライティング解答欄

5

10

15

2022年度第2回　英検準2級　解答用紙

【注意事項】
①解答にはHBの黒鉛筆(シャープペンシルも可)を使用し，解答を訂正する場合には消しゴムで完全に消してください。

②解答用紙は絶対に汚したり折り曲げたり，所定以外のところへの記入はしないでください。

③マーク例

良い例	悪い例
●	

これ以下の濃さのマークは読めません。

解　答　欄

問題番号	1	2	3	4
(1)	①	②	③	④
(2)	①	②	③	④
(3)	①	②	③	④
(4)	①	②	③	④
(5)	①	②	③	④
(6)	①	②	③	④
(7)	①	②	③	④
(8)	①	②	③	④
(9)	①	②	③	④
(10)	①	②	③	④
(11)	①	②	③	④
(12)	①	②	③	④
(13)	①	②	③	④
(14)	①	②	③	④
(15)	①	②	③	④
(16)	①	②	③	④
(17)	①	②	③	④
(18)	①	②	③	④
(19)	①	②	③	④
(20)	①	②	③	④

（問題番号 (1)〜(20) は 1）

解　答　欄

問題番号	1	2	3	4
(21)	①	②	③	④
(22)	①	②	③	④
(23)	①	②	③	④
(24)	①	②	③	④
(25)	①	②	③	④
(26)	①	②	③	④
(27)	①	②	③	④
(28)	①	②	③	④
(29)	①	②	③	④
(30)	①	②	③	④
(31)	①	②	③	④
(32)	①	②	③	④
(33)	①	②	③	④
(34)	①	②	③	④
(35)	①	②	③	④
(36)	①	②	③	④
(37)	①	②	③	④

（(21)〜(25) は 2，(26)〜(30) は 3，(31)〜(37) は 4）

※筆記5の解答欄はこの裏にあります。

リスニング解答欄

問題番号	1	2	3	4
例題	①	②	●	
No.1	①	②	③	
No.2	①	②	③	
No.3	①	②	③	
No.4	①	②	③	
No.5	①	②	③	
No.6	①	②	③	
No.7	①	②	③	
No.8	①	②	③	
No.9	①	②	③	
No.10	①	②	③	
No.11	①	②	③	④
No.12	①	②	③	④
No.13	①	②	③	④
No.14	①	②	③	④
No.15	①	②	③	④
No.16	①	②	③	④
No.17	①	②	③	④
No.18	①	②	③	④
No.19	①	②	③	④
No.20	①	②	③	④
No.21	①	②	③	④
No.22	①	②	③	④
No.23	①	②	③	④
No.24	①	②	③	④
No.25	①	②	③	④
No.26	①	②	③	④
No.27	①	②	③	④
No.28	①	②	③	④
No.29	①	②	③	④
No.30	①	②	③	④

（No.1〜No.10 は 第1部，No.11〜No.20 は 第2部，No.21〜No.30 は 第3部）

※実際の解答用紙に似せていますが，デザイン・サイズは異なります。

●記入上の注意（記述形式）
・指示事項を守り，文字は，はっきりと分かりやすく書いてください。
・太枠に囲まれた部分のみが採点の対象です。

5 ライティング解答欄

5
10
15

2022年度第1回 英検準2級 解答用紙

【注意事項】
①解答にはHBの黒鉛筆（シャープペンシルも可）を使用し，解答を訂正する場合には消しゴムで完全に消してください。
②解答用紙は絶対に汚したり折り曲げたり，所定以外のところへの記入はしないでください。

③マーク例

良い例	悪い例
●	◐ ✗ ◓

 これ以下の濃さのマークは読めません。

解　答　欄

問題番号		1 2 3 4
1	(1)	① ② ③ ④
	(2)	① ② ③ ④
	(3)	① ② ③ ④
	(4)	① ② ③ ④
	(5)	① ② ③ ④
	(6)	① ② ③ ④
	(7)	① ② ③ ④
	(8)	① ② ③ ④
	(9)	① ② ③ ④
	(10)	① ② ③ ④
	(11)	① ② ③ ④
	(12)	① ② ③ ④
	(13)	① ② ③ ④
	(14)	① ② ③ ④
	(15)	① ② ③ ④
	(16)	① ② ③ ④
	(17)	① ② ③ ④
	(18)	① ② ③ ④
	(19)	① ② ③ ④
	(20)	① ② ③ ④

解　答　欄

問題番号		1 2 3 4
2	(21)	① ② ③ ④
	(22)	① ② ③ ④
	(23)	① ② ③ ④
	(24)	① ② ③ ④
	(25)	① ② ③ ④
3	(26)	① ② ③ ④
	(27)	① ② ③ ④
	(28)	① ② ③ ④
	(29)	① ② ③ ④
	(30)	① ② ③ ④
4	(31)	① ② ③ ④
	(32)	① ② ③ ④
	(33)	① ② ③ ④
	(34)	① ② ③ ④
	(35)	① ② ③ ④
	(36)	① ② ③ ④
	(37)	① ② ③ ④

※筆記5の解答欄はこの裏にあります。

リスニング解答欄

問題番号		1 2 3 4
第1部	例題	① ② ●
	No.1	① ② ③
	No.2	① ② ③
	No.3	① ② ③
	No.4	① ② ③
	No.5	① ② ③
	No.6	① ② ③
	No.7	① ② ③
	No.8	① ② ③
	No.9	① ② ③
	No.10	① ② ③
第2部	No.11	① ② ③ ④
	No.12	① ② ③ ④
	No.13	① ② ③ ④
	No.14	① ② ③ ④
	No.15	① ② ③ ④
	No.16	① ② ③ ④
	No.17	① ② ③ ④
	No.18	① ② ③ ④
	No.19	① ② ③ ④
	No.20	① ② ③ ④
第3部	No.21	① ② ③ ④
	No.22	① ② ③ ④
	No.23	① ② ③ ④
	No.24	① ② ③ ④
	No.25	① ② ③ ④
	No.26	① ② ③ ④
	No.27	① ② ③ ④
	No.28	① ② ③ ④
	No.29	① ② ③ ④
	No.30	① ② ③ ④

※実際の解答用紙に似せていますが，デザイン・サイズは異なります。

●記入上の注意（記述形式）
・指示事項を守り，文字は，はっきりと分かりやすく書いてください。
・太枠に囲まれた部分のみが採点の対象です。

5 ライティング解答欄

5
10
15

切り取り線

2021年度第3回　英検準2級　解答用紙

【注意事項】
①解答にはHBの黒鉛筆（シャープペンシルも可）を使用し，解答を訂正する場合には消しゴムで完全に消してください。
②解答用紙は絶対に汚したり折り曲げたり，所定以外のところへの記入はしないでください。

③マーク例

良い例	悪い例
●	◑ ✖ ◔

 これ以下の濃さのマークは読めません。

解　答　欄

問題番号	1	2	3	4
(1)	①	②	③	④
(2)	①	②	③	④
(3)	①	②	③	④
(4)	①	②	③	④
(5)	①	②	③	④
(6)	①	②	③	④
(7)	①	②	③	④
(8)	①	②	③	④
(9)	①	②	③	④
(10)	①	②	③	④
(11)	①	②	③	④
(12)	①	②	③	④
(13)	①	②	③	④
(14)	①	②	③	④
(15)	①	②	③	④
(16)	①	②	③	④
(17)	①	②	③	④
(18)	①	②	③	④
(19)	①	②	③	④
(20)	①	②	③	④

（問題番号1）

解　答　欄

問題番号	1	2	3	4
(21)	①	②	③	④
(22)	①	②	③	④
(23)	①	②	③	④
(24)	①	②	③	④
(25)	①	②	③	④
(26)	①	②	③	④
(27)	①	②	③	④
(28)	①	②	③	④
(29)	①	②	③	④
(30)	①	②	③	④
(31)	①	②	③	④
(32)	①	②	③	④
(33)	①	②	③	④
(34)	①	②	③	④
(35)	①	②	③	④
(36)	①	②	③	④
(37)	①	②	③	④

（問題番号 2：(21)～(25)，3：(26)～(30)，4：(31)～(37)）

※筆記5の解答欄はこの裏にあります。

リスニング解答欄

問題番号	1	2	3	4
例題	①	②	●	
No.1	①	②	③	
No.2	①	②	③	
No.3	①	②	③	
No.4	①	②	③	
No.5	①	②	③	
No.6	①	②	③	
No.7	①	②	③	
No.8	①	②	③	
No.9	①	②	③	
No.10	①	②	③	
No.11	①	②	③	④
No.12	①	②	③	④
No.13	①	②	③	④
No.14	①	②	③	④
No.15	①	②	③	④
No.16	①	②	③	④
No.17	①	②	③	④
No.18	①	②	③	④
No.19	①	②	③	④
No.20	①	②	③	④
No.21	①	②	③	④
No.22	①	②	③	④
No.23	①	②	③	④
No.24	①	②	③	④
No.25	①	②	③	④
No.26	①	②	③	④
No.27	①	②	③	④
No.28	①	②	③	④
No.29	①	②	③	④
No.30	①	②	③	④

（第1部：例題～No.10，第2部：No.11～No.20，第3部：No.21～No.30）

※実際の解答用紙に似せていますが，デザイン・サイズは異なります。

●記入上の注意（記述形式）
・指示事項を守り，文字は，はっきりと分かりやすく書いてください。
・太枠に囲まれた部分のみが採点の対象です。

5 ライティング解答欄

5
10
15

はじめに

実用英語技能検定（英検®）は，年間受験者数420万人（英検IBA，英検Jr.との総数）の小学生から社会人まで，幅広い層が受験する国内最大級の資格試験で，1963年の第1回検定からの累計では1億人を超える人々が受験しています。英検®は，コミュニケーションを行う上で重要となる思考力・判断力・表現力をはじめとして，今日求められている英語能力のあり方に基づいて，2024年度より1〜3級の試験形式の一部をリニューアルする予定です。

この『全問題集シリーズ』は，英語を学ぶ皆さまを応援する気持ちを込めて刊行しました。本書は，2023年度第2回検定を含む6回分の過去問を，皆さまの理解が深まるよう，日本語訳や詳しい解説を加えて収録しています。また，次のページにリニューアルについてまとめていますので，問題に挑戦する前にご確認ください。さらに，「新形式のEメール問題ガイド」も収録していますので，ぜひお役立てください。

本書が皆さまの英検合格の足がかりとなり，さらには国際社会で活躍できるような生きた英語を身につけるきっかけとなることを願っています。

最後に，本書を刊行するにあたり，多大なご尽力をいただきました桐朋中学校・高等学校 秋山安弘先生に深く感謝の意を表します。

2024年　春

2024年度から
英検準2級の試験が変わります!

2024年度第1回検定より, 英検準2級の試験がリニューアルされます。新形式の英作文問題（ライティング）が追加されることが大きなポイントです。リスニングと二次試験（面接）には変更はありません。以下に変更点をまとめました。新試験の概要を把握し, 対策を始めましょう。

リニューアル前の試験			2024年度からの試験		
筆記（75分）			**筆記（80分）** 時間延長		
大問1	短文の語句空所補充	20問	大問1	短文の語句空所補充	15問 → 問題数減
大問2	会話文の文空所補充	5問	大問2	会話文の文空所補充	5問
大問3	長文の語句空所補充	5問	大問3	長文の語句空所補充	2問 → 問題数減
大問4	長文の内容一致選択	7問	大問4	長文の内容一致選択	7問
大問5	英作文（意見論述問題）	1問	大問5	英作文（Eメール問題）	1問 → 1問追加
			大問6	英作文（意見論述問題）	1問

〈変更点〉

筆記	→ 筆記の試験時間が, 75分から80分に延長されます。 → 短文の語句空所補充の問題数が15問に減ります。 → 長文の語句空所補充の問題数が2問に減ります。 → 英作文にEメール問題が追加されます。
リスニング	→ 変更はありません。
面接	→ 変更はありません。

※2023年12月現在の情報を掲載しています。

新形式の Eメール問題ガイド

- あなたは，外国人の知り合い（Alex）から，Eメールで質問を受け取りました。この質問にわかりやすく答える返信メールを，_____に英文で書きなさい。
- あなたが書く返信メールの中で，AlexのEメール文中の下線部について，あなたがより理解を深めるために，下線部の特徴を問う具体的な質問を2つしなさい。
- あなたが書く返信メールの中で_____に書く英文の語数の目安は40語～50語です。
- 解答欄の外に書かれたものは採点されません。
- 解答がAlexのEメールに対応していないと判断された場合は，0点と採点されることがあります。AlexのEメールの内容をよく読んでから答えてください。
- _____の下のBest wishes, の後にあなたの名前を書く必要はありません。

Hi!

Guess what! My father bought me a robot pet last week online. I wanted to get a real dog, but my parents told me it's too difficult to take care of dogs. They suggested that we get a robot dog instead. I'm sending a picture of my robot with this e-mail. My robot is cute, but there's a problem. The battery doesn't last long. Do you think that robot pets will improve in the future?

Your friend,
Alex

Hi, Alex!
Thank you for your e-mail.

解答欄に記入しなさい。

Best wishes,

※英検公式サンプル問題とその模範解答は，公益財団法人 日本英語検定協会の発表によるものです。
　出典：英検ウェブサイト

こんにちは！

ねえねえ，聞いて！　僕の父が先週インターネットで僕にロボットペットを買ってくれたんだ。僕は本物の犬が欲しかったんだけど，両親は犬を世話するのは大変すぎるって言ったんだ。代わりにロボット犬にしたらと言ってくれてね。このEメールと一緒に僕のロボットの写真を送るね。僕のロボットはかわいいけど，困ったことがあるんだ。バッテリーが長く持たないんだよ。君は将来，ロボットペットの性能がもっと良くなると思う？

あなたの友達，
アレックス

こんにちは，アレックス！

Eメールをありがとう。
［解答欄に記入しなさい。］
よろしくね，

模範解答

I'm surprised that you have a robot pet. Do your friends also have robot pets? If so, what kind of animal is popular? About your question, I think robot pets will improve. Think about how much smartphones have changed. They can be used for many hours because of the improvement in technology.

模範解答の訳

君がロボットペットを飼っているとは驚きだよ。君の友達もロボットペットを飼っているの？　もしそうなら，どんな動物が人気なの？　君の質問については，私はロボットペットの性能は良くなると思うよ。スマートフォンがどれだけ変化したか考えてみてよ。技術改良のおかげで長時間使えるもの。

　与えられたEメールは，ロボットの犬のペットを買ってもらったことの報告とそのいきさつ，そして，最後にその問題点としてバッテリーが長く持たないことを挙げ，それと関連してロボットペットの性能が今後向上すると思うかどうかを尋ねている。

　解答はこのEメールへの返信を書くことだが，問題指示文にあるように，下線部（a robot pet）の特徴を問う具体的な質問を2つ書く必要がある。さらにAlexのEメールに対応する内容にするためには，Eメール最後にある質問にも答える必要がある。したがって，解答では，①受信したEメールに対するリアクション→②下線部に関する質問2つ→③Eメールの最終文にある質問に対する回答，の順番で書くという方針を立てることにしよう。

　模範解答の語数は52語である。まず，AlexのEメールへのリアクションだが，模範解答では「ロボットペットを飼っているとは驚きだ」と書いて，ロボット犬についての報告に対する自分の感想を相手に伝えている。今回の報告は相手にとってうれしいことなので，I'm happy to hear [find] (that) ....「…と聞いて［知って］うれしい」やIt's great [wonderful] that ....「…とは素晴らしい」などと喜びを共有する表現を用いることもできる。

　次に2つの質問を書く。a robot petの特徴を問う具体的な質問を書くのだが，模範解答では「君の友達もロボットペットを飼っているのか」と「もしそうなら，どんな動物が人気なのか」の2つが書かれている。外見的な特徴を問うならばWhat color [How big] is your robot pet?「あなたのロボットペットは何色［どのくらいの大きさ］か」などと，機能的な特徴を問うならばCan you feed your robot pet?「ロボットペットにえさをやることができるのか」などと問うこともできる。また，商品としての特徴を問うならばHow much was your robot pet?「ロボットペットはいくらだったのか」などと問うことも可能である。

　最後にAlexの質問に答える。模範解答ではAbout your question「あなたの質問については」で始めて，ここでAlexの質問に回答することをはっきりと示している。そして「ロボットペットの性能は良くなると思う」と明記し，それに続く2文では，根拠としてスマートフォンが技術改良によって長時間使えるようになっていると論じている。このように，質問に答えるときには自分の意見を述べることに加えて，さらにその内容を膨らませるとよい。模範解答のようにその理由を述べることの他に，バッテリーについての問題点が挙げられていたので「あなたはロボットペットを長時間使えるようになるだろう（You will be able to use robot pets for many hours.)」などと具体的に改良されそうな点を述べたり，「ロボットペットはあなたと話せるようにもなるだろう（Robot pets will be able to talk with you, too.)」などさらなる発展の可能性について書いたりしてもよいだろう。

書いた英文を，次の観点からチェック！

☐ 内容…問題文の指示に不足なく答えられているか。
☐ 内容…受け取ったEメールに対する返信として適切な内容か。
☐ 語彙・文法…適切な語彙・文法を用いているか。

- あなたは，外国人の知り合い (Elijah) から，Eメールで質問を受け取りました。この質問に わかりやすく答える返信メールを，☐☐☐☐☐☐☐に英文で書きなさい。
- あなたが書く返信メールの中で，ElijahのEメール文中の下線部について，あなたがより理 解を深めるために，下線部の特徴を問う具体的な質問を2つしなさい。
- あなたが書く返信メールの中で☐☐☐☐☐☐☐に書く英文の語数の目安は40語～50語です。
- 解答欄の外に書かれたものは採点されません。
- 解答がElijahのEメールに対応していないと判断された場合は，0点と採点されることがあ ります。ElijahのEメールの内容をよく読んでから答えてください。
- ☐☐☐☐☐☐☐の下のBest wishes, の後にあなたの名前を書く必要はありません。

Hi!

Guess what! I have started growing vegetables in my garden at home. I wanted to grow apples, but my mom said our garden is too small for an apple tree. She suggested growing vegetables instead. I will give you some of my vegetables when they're ready to eat. Growing vegetables is fun, but it's hard work. I have to give them water every day. Do you think more people will grow vegetables at home in the future?

Your friend,
Elijah

Hi, Elijah!
Thank you for your e-mail.

☐☐☐☐☐☐☐☐☐☐☐☐☐☐☐☐☐☐☐☐☐☐☐☐☐☐☐☐
解答欄に記入しなさい。
☐☐☐☐☐☐☐☐☐☐☐☐☐☐☐☐☐☐☐☐☐☐☐☐☐☐☐☐

Best wishes,

解答欄

	5
	10
	15

こんにちは！

ねえねえ，聞いて！　僕，自宅の庭で野菜を育て始めたんだ。リンゴを育てたかったんだけど，母が自宅の庭はリンゴの木には小さすぎるって言ってね。その代わりに，野菜を育てることを提案してくれたんだ。食べられるようになったら君にも僕の野菜を少しあげるね。野菜栽培は面白いんだけど，それは大変な仕事だよ。毎日水をやらなければならない。君は今後，自宅で野菜を栽培する人が増えると思う？

あなたの友達，
イライジャ

こんにちは，イライジャ！

Eメールをありがとう。
［解答欄に記入しなさい。］
よろしくね，

解答例

It's great that you're growing vegetables in your garden! What vegetables are you growing now? How long does it take for the vegetables to be ready to eat? As for your question, I'm sure more people will enjoy growing vegetables because working outside under the sun is quite refreshing!

解答例の訳

自宅の庭で野菜を育てているなんてすごいね！　君は今，どんな野菜を育てているの？　その野菜が食べられるようになるのにどのくらい時間がかかるのかな？　君の質問については，屋外で太陽の下で作業をすることはとても気持ちがいいから，私は野菜栽培を楽しむ人が絶対に増えると思うよ！

　与えられたEメールは，家庭菜園を始めたことの報告とそれを始めたいきさつを述べ，野菜栽培の面白さと大変さについて触れた後で，今後，家庭菜園をする人が増えると思うかどうかを尋ねている。

　問題指示文にあるように，返信メールには下線部（vegetables in my garden）の特徴を問う具体的な質問を2つ書く必要がある。また，ElijahのEメールに対応している内容にするために，彼のメールの最後にある質問「今後，自宅で野菜を栽培する人が増えると思うか」に答えなければならない。したがって，返信メールの構成として，①受信したEメールに対するリアクション→②下線部に関する質問2つ→③Eメールの最終文にある質問に対する回答，の順番で書くという方針を立てることにする。

　解答例の語数は49語である。まず，受信したEメールへのリアクションだが，解答例では「庭で野菜を育てているとはすごい」と書いて，家庭菜園についての報告に対して自分の感想を相手に伝えている。

　次に2つの質問を書く。vegetables in my garden「庭の野菜」の特徴について具体的な質問を書くことになるが，まず思いつくのは，解答例にあるように，「今はどんな野菜を育てているのか」や「その野菜が食べられるようになるまでにどのくらい時間がかかるのか」ということだろう。他には，「あなたはいくつの野菜を収穫できるのか（How many vegetables can you harvest?）」や「野菜はどんな料理に使われるのか（What kind of dishes can the vegetables be used in?）」なども考えられる。

　最後にElijahの質問に答える。解答例ではAs for your question「あなたの質問については」で始めて，ここでElijahの質問に答えることをはっきりと示している。そして「野菜栽培を楽しむ人は絶対に増えると思う」と自分の考えを書いて，because以下にその理由として「屋外で太陽の下で作業をすることはとても気持ちがいいから」と書いている。このように，自分の考えを述べた後にはその根拠などを書いて，説得力のある内容にしたい。逆の立場の理由としては，「ほとんどの人は仕事などで忙しい（Most people are busy with work and other things.）」や「野菜を育てられる広い庭を持っている人はほとんどいない（Few people have a large garden for growing vegetables.）」なども考えられる。

書いた英文を，次の観点からチェック！

☐ 内容…問題文の指示に不足なく答えられているか。
☐ 内容…受け取ったEメールに対する返信として適切な内容か。
☐ 語彙・文法…適切な語彙・文法を用いているか。

もくじ

Contents

執　筆：秋山 安弘（桐朋中学校・高等学校），Daniel Joyce
編集協力：株式会社 シー・レップス，久島 智津子，入江 泉
録　音：ユニバ合同会社
デザイン：林 慎一郎（及川真咲デザイン事務所）
組版・データ作成協力：幸和印刷株式会社

本書の使い方

ここでは，本書の過去問および特典についての活用法の一例を紹介します。

一次試験対策

情報収集・傾向把握
- 2024年度から英検準2級の試験が変わります！（p.2）
- 英検インフォメーション（p.18-21）
- 2023年度の傾向と攻略ポイント（p.22-23）

予想問題・過去問にチャレンジ
- 新形式のEメール問題ガイド（p.3-9）
- 2023年度第2回一次試験
- 2023年度第1回一次試験
- 2022年度第3回一次試験
- 2022年度第2回一次試験
- 2022年度第1回一次試験
- 2021年度第3回一次試験
  ※アプリ「学びの友」を利用して，自動採点（p.16-17）

二次試験対策

情報収集・傾向把握
- 二次試験・面接の流れ（p.24）
- 【Web特典】
  面接シミュレーション／面接模範例

過去問にチャレンジ
- 2023年度第2回二次試験
- 2023年度第1回二次試験
- 2022年度第3回二次試験
- 2022年度第2回二次試験
- 2022年度第1回二次試験
- 2021年度第3回二次試験

過去問の取り組み方

1セット目
【実力把握モード】
本番の試験と同じように，制限時間を設けて取り組みましょう。どの問題形式に時間がかかりすぎているか，正答率が低いかなど，今のあなたの実力を把握し，学習に生かしましょう。
アプリ「学びの友」の自動採点機能を活用して，答え合わせをスムーズに行いましょう。

2～5セット目
【学習モード】
制限時間をなくし，解けるまで取り組みましょう。
リスニングは音声を繰り返し聞いて解答を導き出してもかまいません。すべての問題に正解できるまで見直します。

6セット目
【仕上げモード】
試験直前の仕上げに利用しましょう。時間を計って本番のつもりで取り組みます。
これまでに取り組んだ6セットの過去問で間違えた問題の解説を本番試験の前にもう一度見直しましょう。

※別冊の解答解説に付いている 正答率 ★75%以上 は，旺文社「英検®一次試験 解答速報サービス」において回答者の正答率が75%以上だった設問を示しています。ぜひ押さえておきたい問題なので，しっかり復習しておきましょう。

音声について

一次試験・リスニングと二次試験・面接の音声を聞くことができます。本書とともに使い，効果的なリスニング・面接対策をしましょう。

収録内容と特長

 ## 一次試験・リスニング

本番の試験の音声を収録	➡	スピードをつかめる！
解答時間は本番通り10秒間	➡	解答時間に慣れる！
収録されている英文は，別冊解答に掲載	➡	聞き取れない箇所を確認できる！

 ## 二次試験・面接（スピーキング）

実際の流れ通りに収録	➡	本番の雰囲気を味わえる！

・パッセージの黙読（試験通り20秒の黙読時間があります）
・パッセージの音読（Model Readingを収録しています）
・質問（音声を一時停止してご利用ください）

各質問のModel Answerも収録	➡	模範解答が確認できる！
Model Answerは，別冊解答に掲載	➡	聞き取れない箇所を確認できる！

12

2つの方法で音声が聞けます！

音声再生 サービス ご利用 可能期間	**2024年2月28日～2025年8月31日** ※ご利用可能期間内にアプリやPCにダウンロードしていただいた音声は，期間終了 　後も引き続きお聞きいただけます。 ※これらのサービスは予告なく変更，終了することがあります。

 ① **公式アプリ「英語の友」**（iOS/Android）で
お手軽再生

リスニング力を強化する機能満載

再生速度変換 （0.5～2.0倍速）	お気に入り機能 （絞込み学習）	オフライン再生

バックグラウンド 再生	試験日 カウントダウン

※画像はイメージです。

［ご利用方法］

1 「英語の友」公式サイトより，アプリをインストール
https://eigonotomo.com/ 　英語の友　🔍
（右の2次元コードから読み込めます）

2 アプリ内のライブラリよりご購入いただいた書籍を選び，
「追加」ボタンを押してください

3 パスワードを入力すると，音声がダウンロードできます
［パスワード：gsvdjz］ ※すべて半角アルファベット小文字

※本アプリの機能の一部は有料ですが，本書の音声は無料でお聞きいただけます。
※詳しいご利用方法は「英語の友」公式サイト，あるいはアプリ内ヘルプをご参照ください。

② パソコンで音声データダウンロード（MP3）

［ご利用方法］

1 Web特典にアクセス　詳細は，p.15をご覧ください。

2 「一次試験［二次試験］音声データダウンロード」から
聞きたい検定の回を選択してダウンロード

※音声ファイルはzip形式にまとめられた形でダウンロードされます。
※音声の再生にはMP3を再生できる機器などが必要です。ご使用機器，音声再生ソフト等に関する技術的なご質問は，ハードメーカーもしくはソフトメーカーにお願いいたします。

CDをご希望の方は，別売「2024年度版英検準2級過去6回全問題集CD」
（本体価格1,500円＋税）をご利用ください。

持ち運びに便利な小冊子とCD3枚付き。　※本書では，収録箇所を**CD 1** **1**～**11**のように表示。

Web特典について

購入者限定の「Web 特典」を，みなさんの英検合格にお役立てください。

ご利用 可能期間	**2024年2月28日〜2025年8月31日** ※本サービスは予告なく変更，終了することがあります。		
アクセス 方法	スマートフォン タブレット	右の2次元コードを読み込むと， パスワードなしでアクセスできます！	
	PC スマートフォン タブレット 共通	1. Web特典（以下のURL）にアクセスします。 　https://eiken.obunsha.co.jp/p2q/ 2. 本書を選択し，以下のパスワードを入力します。 　**gsvdjz**　※すべて半角アルファベット小文字	

〈特典内容〉

(1)解答用紙

本番にそっくりの解答用紙が印刷できるので，何度でも過去問にチャレンジすることができます。

(2)音声データのダウンロード

一次試験リスニング・二次試験面接の音声データ（MP3）を無料でダウンロードできます。

※スマートフォン・タブレットの方は，アプリ「英語の友」(p.13)をご利用ください。

(3)準2級面接対策

【面接シミュレーション】入室から退室までの面接の流れが体験できます。本番の面接と同じ手順で練習ができるので，実際に声に出して練習してみましょう。

【面接模範例】入室から退室までの模範応答例を見ることができます。各チェックポイントで，受験上の注意点やアドバイスを確認しておきましょう。

【問題カード】面接シミュレーションで使用している問題カードです。印刷して，実際の面接の練習に使ってください。

自動採点アプリ「学びの友」の利用方法

本書の問題は，採点・見直し学習アプリ「学びの友」でカンタンに自動採点することができます。

ご利用可能期間	**2024年2月28日～2025年8月31日** ※本サービスは予告なく変更，終了することがあります。 ※ご利用可能期間内にアプリ内で「追加」していた場合は，期間終了後も引き続きお使いいただけます。
アクセス方法	**「学びの友」公式サイトにアクセス** **https://manatomo.obunsha.co.jp/** （右の2次元コードからもアクセスできます）　学びの友　🔍

※iOS／Android端末，Webブラウザよりご利用いただけます。
※アプリの動作環境については，「学びの友」公式サイトをご参照ください。なお，本アプリは無料でご利用いただけます。
※詳しいご利用方法は「学びの友」公式サイト，あるいはアプリ内ヘルプをご参照ください。

［ご利用方法］

1 アプリを起動後，「旺文社まなびID」に会員登録してください
会員登録は無料です。

2 アプリ内の「書籍を追加する」より
ご購入いただいた書籍を選び，「追加」ボタンを押してください

3 パスワードを入力し，コンテンツをダウンロードしてください

パスワード：**gsvdjz**
※すべて半角アルファベット小文字

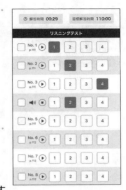

4 学習したい検定回を選択してマークシート を開き，学習を開始します

マークシートを開くと同時にタイマーが動き出します。
問題番号の下には，書籍内掲載ページが表示されています。
問題番号の左側の□に「チェック」を入れることができます。

5 リスニングテストの音声は， 問題番号の横にある再生ボタンをタップ

一度再生ボタンを押したら，最後の問題まで自動的に進みます。

6 リスニングテストが終了したら， 画面右上「採点する」を押して答え合わせをします

※ライティング問題がある級は，「自己採点」ページで模範解答例を参照し，
観点別に自己採点を行ってください。

採点結果の見方

結果画面では，正答率や合格ラインとの距離，間違えた問題の確認ができます。

『問題ごとの正誤』では，プルダウンメニューで，「チェック」した問題，「不正解」の問題，「チェックと不正解」の問題を絞り込んで表示することができますので，解き直しの際にご活用ください。

英検® Information インフォメーション

出典：英検ウェブサイト

英検準2級について

準2級では，「日常生活に必要な英語を理解し，また使用できる」ことが求められます。
入試や単位認定などに幅広く活用されています。
目安としては「高校中級程度」です。

試験内容

一次試験 筆記・リスニング

主な場面・状況	家庭・学校・職場・地域（各種店舗・公共施設を含む）・電話・アナウンスなど
主な話題	学校・趣味・旅行・買い物・スポーツ・映画・音楽・食事・天気・道案内・海外の文化・人物紹介・歴史・教育・科学・自然・環境など

✒ 筆記試験 ⊙ 80分 時間延長

問題	形式・課題詳細	問題数	満点スコア
1	短文の空所に文脈に合う適切な語句を補う。 問題数減	15問	
2	会話文の空所に適切な文や語句を補う。	5問	600
3	パッセージ（長文）の空所に文脈に合う適切な語句を補う。 問題数減	2問	
4	パッセージ（長文）の内容に関する質問に答える。	7問	
5	与えられたEメールに対する返信メールを書く。（40〜50語）NEW	1問	600
6	質問に対して自分の意見とその裏付けとなる理由を書く。（50〜60語）	1問	

🔊 リスニング ⊙ 約25分 放送回数／1回

問題	形式・課題詳細	問題数	満点スコア
第1部	会話の最後の発話に対する応答として最も適切なものを補う。	10問	
第2部	会話の内容に関する質問に答える。	10問	600
第3部	短いパッセージの内容に関する質問に答える。	10問	

2023年12月現在の，2024年度新試験の情報を掲載しています。試験に関する情報は変更になる可能性がありますので，受験の際は必ず英検ウェブサイトをご確認ください。

2024年度から英検準2級が変わります！

1 筆記試験の試験時間が延長されます。
試験時間が，75分から80分になります。

2 語彙問題・長文問題の問題数が削減されます。
大問1は20問から15問になります。また，23年度試験までの3Bがなくなり，大問3は5問から2問になります。

3 英作文問題が1問から2問に増えます。
既存の「意見論述」の問題に加え，「Eメール問題」が出題されます。与えられたEメールに対する返信メールを英語で書きます。語数の目安は40〜50語です。
※Eメール問題の詳細は，「新形式のEメール問題ガイド」（p.3〜）をご参照ください。

二次試験 面接形式のスピーキングテスト

主な場面・題材	日常生活の話題
過去の出題例	ホームシアター・ボランティアガイド・電子辞書・食品フェア・映画祭・プリペイドカードなど

🗨️ スピーキング ⏱ 約6分

問題	形式・課題詳細	満点スコア
音読	50語程度のパッセージを読む。	600
No.1	音読したパッセージの内容についての質問に答える。	
No.2	イラスト中の人物の行動を描写する。	
No.3	イラスト中の人物の状況を説明する。	
No.4	カードのトピックに関連した内容についての質問に答える。	
No.5	日常生活の身近な事柄についての質問に答える。 （カードのトピックに直接関連しない内容も含む）	

合否判定方法

統計的に算出される英検CSEスコアに基づいて合否判定されます。Reading，Writing，Listening，Speakingの4技能が均等に評価され，合格基準スコアは固定されています。

》 技能別にスコアが算出される！

技能	試験形式	満点スコア	合格基準スコア
Reading（読む）	一次試験（筆記1〜4）	600	1322
Writing（書く）	一次試験（筆記5〜6）	600	
Listening（聞く）	一次試験（リスニング）	600	
Speaking（話す）	二次試験（面接）	600	406

● 一次試験の合否は，Reading，Writing，Listeningの技能別にスコアが算出され，それを合算して判定されます。
● 二次試験の合否は，Speakingのみで判定されます。

》 合格するためには，技能のバランスが重要！

英検CSEスコアでは，技能ごとに問題数は異なりますが，スコアを均等に配分しているため，各技能のバランスが重要となります。なお，正答数の目安を提示することはできませんが，2016年度第1回一次試験では，1級，準1級は各技能での正答率が7割程度，2級以下は各技能6割程度の正答率の受験者の多くが合格されています。

》 英検CSEスコアは国際標準規格CEFRにも対応している！

CEFRとは，Common European Framework of Reference for Languages の略。語学のコミュニケーション能力別のレベルを示す国際標準規格。欧米で幅広く導入され，6つのレベルが設定されています。
4技能の英検CSEスコアの合計「4技能総合スコア」と級ごとのCEFR算出範囲に基づいた「4技能総合CEFR」が成績表に表示されます。また，技能別の「CEFRレベル」も表示されます。

CEFR	英検CSEスコア	実用英語技能検定　各級の合格基準スコア
C2	4000〜3300	CEFR算出範囲　　　　　　　　　　　　　　　　　　C1扱い　1級 満点3400
C1	3299〜2600	B2扱い　準1級 満点3000　合格スコア 2630 / 3299
B2	2599〜2300	2級 満点2600　B1扱い　合格スコア 2304 / 2599
B1	2299〜1950	準2級 満点2400　A2扱い　B1扱い 2299　合格スコア 1980 / 1980
A2	1949〜1700	3級 満点2200　A1扱い　合格スコア 1728 / 1949 / 1728
A1	1699〜1400	合格スコア 1456　合格スコア 1728　1699 / 1400 / CEFR算出範囲外
	1399〜0	CEFR算出範囲外　CEFR算出範囲外　1400　CEFR算出範囲外

※ 4級・5級は4技能を測定していないため「4技能総合CEFR」の対象外。
※ 詳しくは英検ウェブサイトをご覧ください。

英検®の種類

英検には，実施方式の異なる複数の試験があります。従来型の英検とその他の英検の問題形式，難易度，級認定，合格証明書発行，英検CSEスコア取得等はすべて同じです。

英検®（従来型）

紙の問題冊子を見て解答用紙に解答。二次試験を受験するためには，一次試験に合格する必要があります。

英検 S-CBT

コンピュータを使って受験。1日で4技能を受験することができ，原則，毎週土日に実施されています（級や地域により毎週実施でない場合があります）。

英検 S-Interview

点字や吃音等，CBT方式では対応が難しい受験上の配慮が必要な方のみ受験可能。

※受験する級によって選択できる方式が異なります。各方式の詳細および最新情報は英検ウェブサイト（https://www.eiken.or.jp/eiken/）をご確認ください。

英検®（従来型）受験情報

※「従来型・本会場」以外の実施方式については，試験日程・申込方法が異なりますので，英検ウェブサイトをご覧ください。
※受験情報は変更になる場合があります。

◉ 2024年度 試験日程

	第1回	第2回	第3回
申込受付	3月15日▶5月8日	7月1日▶9月9日	11月1日▶12月16日
一次試験	6月 2日（日）	10月 6日（日）	2025年 1月26日（日）
二次試験	A 7月 7日（日） B 7月14日（日）	A 11月10日（日） B 11月17日（日）	A 2025年 3月 2日（日） B 2025年 3月 9日（日）

※上記の申込期間はクレジット支払いの場合。支払い・申し込みの方法によって締切日が異なるのでご注意ください。
※一次試験は上記以外の日程でも準会場で受験できる可能性があります。
※二次試験にはA日程，B日程があり，年齢などの条件により指定されます。
※詳しくは英検ウェブサイトをご覧ください。

◉ 申込方法

団体受験 学校や塾などで申し込みをする団体受験もあります。詳しくは先生にお尋ねください。

個人受験 インターネット申込・コンビニ申込・英検特約書店申込のいずれかの方法で申し込みができます。詳しくは英検ウェブサイトをご覧ください。

お問い合わせ先

英検サービスセンター	英検ウェブサイト
TEL.03-3266-8311	www.eiken.or.jp/eiken/
㊊～㊎ 9：30～17：00 （祝日・年末年始を除く）	詳しい試験情報を見たり，入試等で英検を活用している学校を検索したりすることができます。

2023年度の傾向と攻略ポイント

英検準 2 級は 2024 年度第 1 回検定から試験形式が一部変わります。ここでは，旧試験である 2023 年度第 1 回検定と第 2 回検定の分析をまとめています。あらかじめご了承ください。

一次試験　筆記（75分）

1　短文の語句空所補充

1〜2 文程度の長さから成る文の空所に入る適切な語句を選ぶ。

問題数 **20** 問
めやす **12** 分

傾向
単語 名詞 4 問，動詞 4〜5 問のほか，形容詞や副詞の出題。やや難易度の高い refuse（第 1 回 (6)）や strike の過去形 struck（第 2 回 (1)）などが出題された。

熟語 全部で 7 問。後ろに -ing 形をとる take turns *doing*（第 1 回 (11)）や each other の同意表現である one another（第 2 回 (15)）などが出題された。

文法 過去完了の大過去の意味での用法，関係副詞 where，時を表す副詞節内での時制，主語の位置の nobody，enjoy *doing*，前置詞 above などが出題された。

攻略ポイント 単語・熟語では，派生語や関連表現もあわせておさえたい。文法では，仮定法や受動態，不定詞・動名詞・分詞など動詞に関する項目，関係詞が特に重要である。

2　会話文の文空所補充

A・B，2 人の会話文の空所に適切な文や語句を補う。

問題数 **5** 問
めやす **8** 分

傾向 ほとんどの場合，選択肢は文の一部であり，解答の決め手となる部分は空所の後に出てくる。また，全体から話題となっているものを考えさせる問題もある。

攻略ポイント 解答の基本は，空所前までで会話の状況を把握し，空所後から判断の根拠を探す。また，空所後にある代名詞が指すものを選択肢の中から見つける問題もある。

3　長文の語句空所補充

[A] 150 語程度，[B] 250 語程度の長文の空所に適切な語句を補う。

問題数 **5** 問
めやす **15** 分

傾向 選択肢は複数語から成り，主語の後に続く動詞で始まる部分がほとんどだが，不定詞の to の後や動詞の長めの目的語（の一部），接続表現そのもののこともある。

攻略ポイント 各段落の中心的内容をつかみ，文章全体の展開を捉えよう。空所前後の文は特に丁寧に読み，文脈から空所部分の意味を予測してから選択肢を選ぶのがコツ。

4　長文の内容一致選択

[A] 200 語程度，[B] 300 語程度の長文の内容に関する質問に答える。

問題数 **7** 問
めやす **20** 分

傾向 各段落について 1 問ずつ出題される。[A] は個人的なメール，[B] は社会的・科学的な内容（第 1 回はゲームセンター，第 2 回はドライブインシアター）である。

攻略ポイント まず，質問の語句を手がかりに，問われている部分を本文中から探す。解答のカギはたいていその前後にあるので注意して読む。段落ごとに解答してもよい。

| **5** | **英作文**
質問に対する回答を英文で書く。 | 問題数 **1**問
めやす **20**分 |

傾向　質問は，賛成・反対を問うものが基本だが二者選択もある。第1回では週末の病院開院の是非，第2回では夏休みに学習計画を立てることの是非が問われた。

**攻略
ポイント**　「意見（立場表明）」→「理由2つ」→「まとめ」という基本的な英文構成を意識する。理由は2文程度に膨らませて書き，自分の選んだ立場を支持する内容でなければならない。表現の繰り返しを避け，バリエーションにも配慮したい。

 一次試験　リスニング（約25分）

| 第 **1** 部 | **会話の応答文選択** | 会話の最後の発話に対する応答として最も適
切なものを補う。 | 問題数 **10**問 |

傾向　文脈から会話の最後の発言に対して適切な応答や感想を選ぶ問題と，最後が疑問文でそれに対する適切な答えを選ぶ問題がおおよそ半々である。

**攻略
ポイント**　最初のやりとりから，この会話が誰と誰の会話で，どんな状況であるのかをすばやくつかもう。道案内や店，レストランでの会話，電話での問い合わせなどの典型的なやりとりについては，普段から意識して定型表現をおさえておきたい。

| 第 **2** 部 | **会話の内容一致選択** | 会話の内容に関する質問に答える。 | 問題数 **10**問 |
| 第 **3** 部 | **文の内容一致選択** | 短い文章の内容に関する質問に答える。 | 問題数 **10**問 |

傾向　第2部では，友人・親子・夫婦などの会話の他に，図書館や商店での会話が出題された。電話での会話も2問程度出る。第3部では，ある人物の体験・出来事の話が過半数を占めるが，他に「アフリカの小動物ガラゴ（第1回）」や「印刷ミスのある切手（第2回）」の説明，乗客や受験生への案内が出題された。

**攻略
ポイント**　会話の状況と話のトピックをすばやく理解し，話の展開をつかんだ上で，質問を正確に聞き取るのがコツ。余裕があれば，放送が始まる前に選択肢に目を通しておくとよい。質問を予想した上でポイントを絞って聞くと効率良く解答できる。

 二次試験　面接（約6分）

英語の文章と2つのイラストの描かれたカードが渡される。20秒の黙読の後，文章の音読をするよう指示される。それから5つの質問がされる。

No. 1 文章に関する質問。by doing so や in this way などが指す部分を見抜くのがカギ。

No. 2 イラストAに描かれた人物の5つの動作について，現在進行形を用いて説明する。

No. 3 イラストBの人物について，解答のポイントを2点読み取り，説明する。

No. 4 音読した文章に関連した内容で，今後の社会状況などについての一般的な質問に対して意見を問う質問。Yes / No と答えた後，その理由などを2文程度で説明する。

No. 5 身近な事項について受験者自身の好みや習慣などを問う質問。No. 4と同じく，ペアクエスチョン。声の大きさや明瞭さ，積極性などの面接に向かう姿勢にも気を配りたい。

二次試験・面接の流れ

（1）入室とあいさつ

係員の指示に従い，面接室に入ります。あいさつをしてから，面接委員に面接カードを手渡し，指示に従って，着席しましょう。

（2）氏名と受験級の確認

面接委員があなたの氏名と受験する級の確認をします。その後，簡単なあいさつをしてから試験開始です。

（3）問題カードの黙読

英文とイラストが印刷された問題カードを手渡されます。まず，英文を20秒で黙読するよう指示されます。英文の分量は50語程度です。

※問題カードには複数の種類があり，面接委員によっていずれか1枚が手渡されます。本書では英検協会から提供を受けたもののみ掲載しています。

（4）問題カードの音読

英文の音読をするように指示されるので，英語のタイトルから読みましょう。時間制限はないので，意味のまとまりごとにポーズをとり，焦らずにゆっくりと読みましょう。

（5）5つの質問

音読の後，面接委員の5つの質問に答えます。No.1～3は問題カードの英文とイラストについての質問です。No.4・5は受験者自身の意見を問う質問です。No.3の質問の後，カードを裏返すように指示されるので，No.4・5は面接委員を見ながら話しましょう。

（6）カード返却と退室

試験が終了したら，問題カードを面接委員に返却し，あいさつをして退室しましょう。

2023-2

一次試験 2023.10.8実施
二次試験 Ａ日程 2023.11. 5 実施
　　　　 Ｂ日程 2023.11.12実施

Grade Pre-2

Pre 2

試験時間

筆記：75分

リスニング：約25分

＊解答・解説は別冊p.5〜40にあります。
＊面接の流れは本書p.24にあります。

1 次の **(1)** から **(20)** までの（　　　）に入れるのに最も適切なものを **1**, **2**, **3**, **4** の中から一つ選び，その番号を解答用紙の所定欄にマークしなさい。

(1) Ryuji's teammate passed the soccer ball to Ryuji. He (　　) the ball as hard as he could, and it flew past the goalkeeper and into the goal.

1 mixed　　　　**2** chewed　　　　**3** struck　　　　**4** copied

(2) *A:* Dad, I don't feel well. My head hurts and I think I have a (　　).

B: I see. Let me check your temperature.

1 grade　　　　**2** surprise　　　　**3** custom　　　　**4** fever

(3) Most companies use ships to (　　) their products overseas. Airplanes are much faster, but they are usually much more expensive.

1 transport　　　**2** design　　　**3** consult　　　**4** reject

(4) After the basketball game, Mark's coach said many nice things about his passing and defense. He felt (　　) to hear that he was doing a good job.

1 frightened　　**2** encouraged　　**3** delivered　　**4** followed

(5) *A:* How long have you been working here, Sabrina?
B: I'm new. I was (　　) two weeks ago.

1 collected　　**2** hired　　　**3** exchanged　　**4** carried

(6) Kansai is a (　　) in western Japan. Its three largest cities are Osaka, Kyoto, and Kobe.

1 safety　　　**2** region　　　**3** theme　　　**4** laundry

(7) *A:* Could you answer all the questions in our math homework?
B: Nearly. I couldn't (　　) the last one, though.

1 solve　　　**2** repair　　　**3** miss　　　**4** invent

(8) Kelly writes two ( ) every month for her English class. Last month, she wrote about a book that she had recently read and what she did during the summer vacation.
1 essays   **2** victories   **3** systems   **4** miracles

(9) There is a store by Lucy's house that sells clothes very ( ). On Saturday, Lucy bought a blouse there for only $10.
1 powerfully   **2** lately   **3** bravely   **4** cheaply

(10) David became very rich after he created a popular smartphone app. He uses most of his ( ) to help people who do not have much money.
1 pain   **2** wealth   **3** nonsense   **4** literature

(11) Lester could not go to school for three days last week because he was ( ) a bad cold. He feels much better this week.
1 suffering from   **2** depending on
3 giving up   **4** majoring in

(12) *A:* I'm sorry I didn't hear your question, Ms. Nakayama.
    B: Please ( ), Asako. You can't learn if you don't listen in class!
1 shake hands   **2** make sense   **3** take turns   **4** pay attention

(13) A tree had fallen on the train line to Karinville. Passengers traveling there had to take buses ( ) of trains until the problem was fixed.
1 on behalf   **2** for fear   **3** by way   **4** in place

(14) *A:* Excuse me. I think you have my suitcase.
    B: Oh, sorry! I must have taken it ( ). It looks just like mine.
1 at present   **2** by mistake   **3** for nothing   **4** with ease

(15) Tetsuya has a Canadian friend called Todd. Tetsuya and Todd write to ( ) at least once a month.
1 any other   **2** one another   **3** every other   **4** another one

(16) *A:* Do you know whether your baby will be a boy or a girl?
   B: No, not yet. My husband and I are (   ) a girl because our first child is a boy.

   1 hoping for   **2** taking over
   3 putting away   **4** showing off

(17) Tom and Helen both wanted to get a puppy, but they could not (   ) a name for it. Tom wanted to call it Buddy, but Helen wanted to call it Max.

   1 pour out   **2** agree on   **3** run over   **4** hold up

(18) Mr. Smirnov has to have his monthly report done by the time his boss (   ) back to the office.

   1 come   **2** comes   **3** came   **4** will come

(19) The other day, James went to the town (   ) he was born. It had been a few years since his last visit, but the town had not changed much.

   1 when   **2** where   **3** why   **4** which

(20) A beautiful blue bird was flying (   ) the tree in Paul's garden. Paul wanted to take a picture of it, but it quickly flew away.

   1 of   **2** on   **3** above   **4** among

2 次の四つの会話文を完成させるために，(21) から (25) に入るものとして最も適切なものを 1，2，3，4 の中から一つ選び，その番号を解答用紙の所定欄にマークしなさい。

(21) *A:* Is the restaurant still open?
　　B: Yes, but (　**21**　).
　　A: Oh no! I had to work late, and I couldn't get anything to eat.
　　B: There's a place that sells hamburgers up the street. I think it's open 24 hours.

　　1 we only have a table for two people
　　2 the last order was 10 minutes ago
　　3 it's the chef's first day here today
　　4 we have run out of ice cream

----

(22) *A:* Hi, Bob. Is that (　**22**　)? It's really cool.
　　B: Yes. I got it at the department store by the station.
　　A: Was it expensive?
　　B: Not really. The sports and games department is having a big sale this month.

　　1 a gold ring
　　2 a new skateboard
　　3 your brother's car
　　4 your new lunch box

----

(23) *A:* Excuse me. I (　**23**　).
　　B: Certainly, ma'am. We have many different kinds. Which would you like?
　　A: I'm not sure. The one I have now makes my neck hurt.
　　B: It could be too soft. Try this one and tell me if it's as soft as yours.

　　1 want a new pillow for my bed
　　2 would like to get a new necklace
　　3 need a new carpet for my hall
　　4 am looking for a new paintbrush

A: Would you like one of these cookies?

B: Yes, please. They're so pretty! Where did you get them?

A: (　**24**　).

B: I didn't know you had visited there.

A: Yes. My family and I went for a week. We got back to London last night.

B: I wish that I could go there someday.

A: You should. There are (　**25**　).

B: I know. I saw a TV program about the museums and palaces there.

(24) **1** At a shop in Paris
     2 From an online bakery
     3 I made them myself
     4 My grandma sent them to me

(25) **1** only a few seats left
     2 some great places to see
     3 six different flavors
     4 several ways to make them

（筆記試験の問題は次のページに続きます。）

次の英文 [A], [B] を読み，その文意にそって (26) から (30) までの (　　) に入れるのに最も適切なものを 1, 2, 3, 4 の中から一つ選び，その番号を解答用紙の所定欄にマークしなさい。

[A]

Stephen's New School

Stephen's family recently moved to a new city, and Stephen had to change schools. He did not know anyone at his new school, and he felt lonely every day. He (**26**) about his problem. Stephen's mother said that he would make new friends soon, and his father suggested joining one of the clubs at his new school. However, Stephen did not like sports, music, or art, so he did not know what to do.

One day, Stephen saw a poster at school for a games club. The members met three times a week to play board games and card games. Stephen really liked playing games, so he joined the club. The members were very kind, and Stephen quickly made friends. Recently, Stephen decided to (**27**). He has been working hard to make the rules and the other things he will need for the game. Once it is ready, he plans to try it with the other members of the club.

(26) **1** read several books **2** wrote a long letter
 3 saw a doctor **4** talked to his parents
(27) **1** create his own game **2** join another club
 3 change schools again **4** get more exercise

[B] *The Return of Greeting Cards*

During the 20th century, people often sent paper greeting cards to friends and family members on birthdays or at other special times. Greeting cards usually have a picture on the front and a message inside. In the 1990s, however, people began communicating online. Sending an electronic message by e-mail or through social media is quicker and easier than sending a paper greeting card. In addition, most greeting cards are thrown away. This creates a lot of trash. As a result, some people prefer online communication because they think it is (**28**).

For several years, sales of greeting cards in the United States went down. Recently, though, young adults have become interested in greeting cards. Many of them think that it is too easy to send a message online. Sending a greeting card to a person (**29**). It shows that you really care about that person. Because of this, Americans still buy around 6.5 billion greeting cards every year.

Although people once thought that the Internet might be bad for sales of greeting cards, it may actually be helping them. This is because people who use social media are often (**30**). For example, they may be sent a message to tell them that one of their friends has a birthday or wedding anniversary soon. As a result, they remember to buy a greeting card and send it to their friend.

(28) 1 easier to talk in private

2 better for the environment

3 creating many jobs

4 new and exciting

(29) 1 takes more effort

2 can lead to problems

3 is not always possible

4 may not change anything

(30) 1 invited to play games   2 sent photos of food

3 reminded about events   4 shown advertisements

[A]

From: Henry Robbins <h-g-robbins@oldmail.com>
To: Peter Robbins <peter1512@whichmail.com>
Date: October 8
Subject: My visit

Dear Peter,

I'm really excited to see you again next week. I had such a great week the last time that I visited. I can't believe it's been 12 months already. I'm glad I can stay for a whole month this time. I'm planning lots of fun things for us to do together. Please tell your little sister that I'm looking forward to playing with her again, too.

I thought we could go camping by Mirror Lake. We could try fishing in the lake, too. Have you ever been fishing before? I took your dad fishing many times when he was a boy. It's very relaxing, but you have to be ready and move quickly if you want to catch anything! I can teach you lots of tricks to help you become a good fisher.

I also thought that we could go to watch a baseball game together. I haven't been to any big baseball games for a long time because there aren't any professional teams near my house. Your dad told me that you joined a baseball team in your town a few months ago. How is that going? If you want to, we can go to a park to practice throwing, catching, and hitting.

Anyway, I'll see you very soon.

Love,

Grandpa

(31) What is one thing that Grandpa says to Peter?

1 It is not possible for him to stay for longer than a week.
2 It has been a year since he last visited Peter.
3 He cannot wait to meet Peter's sister for the first time.
4 He will visit Peter's house in about one month.

(32) Grandpa asks Peter

1 whether he can run quickly.
2 whether he has ever gone fishing.
3 if he knows how to do any magic tricks.
4 if he has gone camping before.

(33) What did Peter start doing recently?

1 Playing for a local sports team.
2 Going to professional baseball games.
3 Taking his sister to play in the park.
4 Learning about history at school.

[B]
Drive-in Movie Theaters

Richard Hollingshead was an American businessman. His mother loved movies, but she did not like the hard seats in movie theaters. Hollingshead thought that she might be more comfortable if she could watch movies while sitting on the soft seats of her own car. He put a screen and some speakers in his yard and invited his family and neighbors to try his new business idea: a drive-in movie theater.

Hollingshead opened a bigger drive-in movie theater in 1933, but he did not make much money from it. Other people copied his idea, though, and drive-in movie theaters soon became popular, especially with people with small children. One reason was that the children could run around and shout without bothering other people. Some drive-in movie theaters even had playgrounds, so children could enjoy themselves while they waited for the movies to start.

At first, these theaters had large speakers near the screen. The sound was not good, so some theaters put a speaker by every car. However, there were other problems for drive-in movie theaters. One was that drive-in movie theaters could only show movies in the evening after it became dark. Also, movie companies got more money from indoor theaters, so many of them did not let drive-in movie theaters show their best movies. Drive-in movie theaters often had to show movies that were older or less popular.

In the 1970s, many drive-in movie theaters closed because people could rent videos to watch at home. Also, many drive-in movie theaters were just outside large towns and cities. Companies wanted the theaters so that they could build new homes on the land. They offered the owners a lot of money, and many owners decided to sell their theaters. Although there were over 4,000 drive-in movie theaters in the United States around 1960, today, there are just a few hundred left.

(34) What is one thing that we learn about Richard Hollingshead's mother?

    1 She made a drive-in movie theater in her yard.
    2 She learned how to drive a car by watching movies.
    3 She often held parties for her family and neighbors.
    4 She thought movie theater seats were not comfortable.

(35) One reason that drive-in movie theaters became popular was

    1 they offered special discounts to families with children.
    2 parents did not have to worry if their children were noisy.
    3 most indoor movie theaters did not show movies for children.
    4 many of them were built near parks with children's playgrounds.

(36) Some movies were not shown in drive-in movie theaters because

    1 it was too dark in the evening to see the movies easily.
    2 the sound in the movies was not good enough.
    3 movie companies made more money from indoor theaters.
    4 they had not been popular in indoor theaters.

(37) Why did many drive-in movie theater owners sell their theaters?

    1 Companies offered to pay them a lot of money for their land.
    2 The theaters were too far away from large towns and cities.
    3 They wanted to open stores so that people could rent videos.
    4 People started making drive-in theaters in their own yards.

5

●あなたは，外国人の知り合いから以下の **QUESTION** をされました。

● **QUESTION** について，あなたの意見とその<u>理由を 2 つ</u>英文で書きなさい。

●語数の目安は **50** 語～**60** 語です。

●解答は，解答用紙の **B** 面にあるライティング解答欄に書きなさい。<u>なお，解答欄の外に書かれたものは採点されません。</u>

●解答が **QUESTION** に対応していないと判断された場合は，<u>0 点と採点されることがあります。</u> **QUESTION** をよく読んでから答えてください。

QUESTION

Do you think it is good for students to make study plans for their summer vacations?

（リスニングテストは次のページにあります。）

リスニング

準2級リスニングテストについて

1 このリスニングテストには，第1部から第3部まであります。
☆英文はすべて一度しか読まれません。
第1部：対話を聞き，その最後の文に対する応答として最も適切なものを，放送される
1，2，3の中から一つ選びなさい。
第2部：対話を聞き，その質問に対して最も適切なものを1，2，3，4の中から一つ選
びなさい。
第3部：英文を聞き，その質問に対して最も適切なものを1，2，3，4の中から一つ選
びなさい。
2 No. 30のあと，10秒すると試験終了の合図がありますので，筆記用具を置いてください。

||||| 第1部 ||||| 🔊 ▶MP3 ▶アプリ ▶CD1 **1**～**11**

No. 1～No. 10（選択肢はすべて放送されます。）

||||| 第2部 ||||| 🔊 ▶MP3 ▶アプリ ▶CD1 **12**～**22**

No. 11
1 It has a lot of customers.
2 It closed last night.
3 They do not serve steak.
4 They do not have a website.

No. 12
1 Getting ready to go to the supermarket.
2 Trying out a Japanese recipe.
3 Making a dish from her hometown.
4 Learning how to make beef stew.

No. 13
1 She needs help with schoolwork.
2 She will not be on time for dinner.
3 She was not in math class today.
4 She wants to start learning karate.

No. 14	1 It looks damaged.
	2 It can only use old software.
	3 It has been used by many people.
	4 It is not old enough.

No. 15	1 To return a ring.
	2 To meet the store owner.
	3 To buy some earrings.
	4 To get her watch fixed.

No. 16	1 Invite a friend to dinner.
	2 Eat dinner before he leaves home.
	3 Make pasta for his mother.
	4 Go to the theater to see a movie.

No. 17	1 To tell her about drink prices.
	2 Which drinks use chocolate.
	3 About coffee drinks without milk.
	4 How the drinks are made.

No. 18	1 She did not study for her science test.
	2 She did not sleep well last night.
	3 She does not have time for homework.
	4 She does not do well in science.

No. 19	1 He cannot work tonight.
	2 He does not like pizza.
	3 He canceled his order.
	4 He called the wrong number.

No. 20	1 He does not like his shirt.
	2 He cannot find his shirt.
	3 His brother made his shirt dirty.
	4 His shirt is too big.

No. 21
1 A math teacher.
2 A nurse.
3 A biology teacher.
4 A doctor.

No. 22
1 Paula gave him a soccer ball.
2 Paula came to his soccer match.
3 Paula stopped learning ballet.
4 Paula met a famous ballet dancer.

No. 23
1 He helped Jonathan to swim faster.
2 He taught Jonathan how to dive.
3 He let Jonathan use his stopwatch.
4 He gave Jonathan a ride to his race.

No. 24
1 Over one million copies of them were stolen.
2 They were bought by a famous photographer.
3 A new type of machine was used to print them.
4 There was a mistake made with the pictures.

No. 25
1 It will take place this Sunday.
2 Six of Zack's friends planned it.
3 He cannot go bowling on that day.
4 Zack's parents cannot go to it.

No. 26
1 She helped him study for an important test.
2 She agreed to take him to see a doctor.
3 She fixed his bike after he broke it.
4 She let him use her phone to make a call.

No. 27
1 By asking one of the Grade 10 students.
2 By asking someone in Classroom 204.
3 By checking the list by the main entrance.
4 By checking their examinee forms.

No. 28

1 The flavor of his onions was too strong.
2 Somebody put peppers into his food.
3 His potatoes took too long to grow.
4 A rabbit ate some of his vegetables.

No. 29

1 It was designed to look like a mountain.
2 It was built more than 2,000 years ago.
3 It was named after a famous musician.
4 It was created after a market closed down.

No. 30

1 She does not need to work part-time anymore.
2 She does not always have to ride her bike to college.
3 She has more time to spend on her studies.
4 She has enough money to buy a new bike.

Studying Abroad Online

Today, many people study abroad. However, it sometimes takes a lot of time and money to go to other countries. Now, technology is playing an important role. Some people take online classes that are held by foreign schools, and by doing so they can experience studying abroad without leaving their own countries.

A

B

Questions

No. 1   According to the passage, how can some people experience studying abroad without leaving their own countries?

No. 2   Now, please look at the people in Picture A. They are doing different things. Tell me as much as you can about what they are doing.

No. 3   Now, look at the girl in Picture B. Please describe the situation.

Now, Mr. / Ms. ____, please turn over the card and put it down.

No. 4   Do you think junior high schools should offer more cooking classes for their students?
Yes. → Why?
No. → Why not?

No. 5   Today, many people take a shopping bag when they go to the supermarket. Do you take your own shopping bag to the supermarket?
Yes. → Please tell me more.
No. → Why not?

Online Discount Stores

Today, discount stores on the Internet are attracting attention. People can buy things at lower prices, and as a result they find online discount stores helpful. However, people in some areas can have trouble using them. For example, they need to wait a long time for products to be delivered.

A

B

Questions

No. 1 According to the passage, why do people find online discount stores helpful?

No. 2 Now, please look at the people in Picture A. They are doing different things. Tell me as much as you can about what they are doing.

No. 3 Now, look at the woman in Picture B. Please describe the situation.

Now, Mr. / Ms. _____, please turn over the card and put it down.

No. 4 Do you think using the Internet is a good way for people to learn English?
Yes. → Why?
No. → Why not?

No. 5 Today, there are many kinds of restaurants. Do you like to eat at restaurants?
Yes. → Please tell me more.
No. → Why not?

2023-1

一次試験 2023.6.4 実施
二次試験 Ａ日程 2023.7.2 実施
　　　　 Ｂ日程 2023.7.9 実施

Grade Pre-2

Pre

2

試験時間

筆記：75分
リスニング：約25分

＊解答・解説は別冊p.41〜76にあります。
＊面接の流れは本書p.24にあります。

1 次の (1) から (20) までの （　　　） に入れるのに最も適切なものを 1, 2, 3, 4 の中から一つ選び，その番号を解答用紙の所定欄にマークしなさい。

(1) The teacher (　　　) his notes from the blackboard before Ruth was able to finish copying them into her notebook. She had to ask another student for help.
  1 erased　　　**2** excused　　　**3** escaped　　　**4** extended

(2) *A:* Why did you cancel the picnic? I was looking forward to it.
  B: So was I, but it's going to rain. We have no (　　　) over the weather.
  1 issue　　　**2** grade　　　**3** fever　　　**4** control

(3) *A:* It's really cold this winter, isn't it?
  B: I know! I have four (　　　) on my bed, and I am still cold at night.
  1 locks　　　**2** blankets　　　**3** moments　　　**4** husbands

(4) The new TV show *Amazing Plants* is very (　　　). Children who watch it can learn about lots of strange plants.
  1 modern　　　**2** lonely　　　**3** violent　　　**4** educational

(5) Mr. Suzuki's vacation in Hawaii was like a wonderful dream. However, he knew that he would have to go back to the (　　　) of his job in Tokyo.
  1 origin　　　**2** suggestion　　　**3** reality　　　**4** coast

(6) Wesley offered to buy Sarah's guitar from her, but she (　　　). She did not want to sell it because it was a gift from her father.
  1 employed　　　**2** existed　　　**3** retired　　　**4** refused

(7) Andrew looks forward to visiting his grandparents on the weekend because he always has interesting (　　　) with them. They always talk about history.
  1 consumers　　**2** approaches　　**3** muscles　　　**4** discussions

(8) Simon's homework is to write about someone who he (　　). Simon has decided to write about his favorite baseball player because he is Simon's hero.

1 respects　　**2** locates　　**3** assists　　**4** combines

(9) When Dennis arrived at his aunt's house, she (　　) him at the door with a hug.

1 greeted　　**2** promised　　**3** required　　**4** interviewed

(10) *A:* I think you're sitting in the seat that I reserved.
B: Oh! I'm (　　) sorry. I'll find somewhere else to sit.

1 equally　　**2** terribly　　**3** calmly　　**4** safely

(11) Casey and his sister (　　) washing the dishes. He washes them after breakfast and she washes them after dinner.

1 take turns　　　　　　**2** give applause
3 pass around　　　　　**4** have faith

(12) Alan went to Hawaii last week, but he could not enjoy any of the beaches because he was there (　　).

1 at least　　**2** by heart　　**3** for good　　**4** on business

(13) After work on Friday night, Jason did not want to cook at home. He (　　) having dinner with his friends, so he invited three of them to a restaurant.

1 looked like　　**2** felt like　　**3** passed by　　**4** ran by

(14) *A:* Gina, could I go to one of your photography club meetings and see what it's like?
B: Sure. Our meetings (　　) on the first Saturday of each month.

1 take place　　**2** grow up　　**3** come true　　**4** put off

(15) After Suzanne graduated from college, she did not plan to (　　) her parents. She got a job so she could live by herself.

1 lay out　　**2** rely on　　**3** turn in　　**4** get over

(16) *A:* What are you going to wear at the Christmas party?

B: I'm going to (   ) as a snowman. My mom is helping me to make my costume.

1 turn off   **2** hold back   **3** dress up   **4** break out

(17) Dan gave a presentation in his science class today. He (   ) his main ideas with data from research.

1 pulled away **2** called out   **3** wished for   **4** backed up

(18) Mike cried when he broke the toy truck that his mother (   ) him for his birthday.

1 has given   **2** was giving   **3** was given   **4** had given

(19) Bobby wanted to play catch, so he asked his parents, his brother, and his sister if they had time to play with him. However, (   ) did because they were all too busy.

1 nobody   **2** everybody   **3** anybody   **4** somebody

(20) On Saturdays, Beth volunteers at her local community center. She enjoys (   ) with events for the people in her area.

1 to help   **2** helps   **3** helping   **4** helped

2 次の四つの会話文を完成させるために, **(21)** から **(25)** に入るものとして最も適切なものを 1, 2, 3, 4 の中から一つ選び, その番号を解答用紙の所定欄にマークしなさい。

---

(21) *A:* Here is your room key, sir. You're in Room 403 on the fourth floor.

B: Is there anywhere that I can (**21**)?

A: You should find some bottles of water in the fridge in your room, and there's also a vending machine here in the lobby, sir.

B: Thanks!

1 leave my bags for a few hours
2 find out more about the city
3 buy an English newspaper
4 get something to drink

---

(22) *A:* Are you leaving already?

B: Yes. I want to be home by 7:30 so that I can (**22**).

A: Oh, is that tonight? I forgot about that.

B: It's going to be really exciting. It's between the two best teams in the world.

1 watch the international rugby game
2 make dinner for my wife
3 read a bedtime story to my kids
4 take a bath and go to bed early

---

(23) *A:* Hi. Do you have (**23**) in the library?

B: Yes. Do you want to see photos of famous ones?

A: No. I want to find out how to grow bigger vegetables.

B: In that case, try looking in section E3 on the second floor.

1 books about movie actors
2 anything about gardens
3 advice about food shopping
4 information about paintings

A: Honey, have you seen my smartphone? I can't find it anywhere.

B: No, I haven't. Do you want me to (24   )?

A: Yes, please. Hopefully, we'll be able to hear where it is.

B: OK. It's ringing now.

A: I can hear it. The sound is coming from (25   ).

B: How did it get there?

A: I must have left it there by accident when I was putting away the food we bought at the supermarket.

B: Well, I'm glad that we've found it.

(24) **1** buy a new one for you
2 set an alarm
3 try calling it
4 search upstairs

(25) **1** under the bed
2 one of the kitchen cabinets
3 behind the bookshelves
4 the laundry basket

（筆記試験の問題は次のページに続きます。）

3 次の英文 [A], [B] を読み，その文意にそって (26) から (30) までの (　　) に入れるのに最も適切なものを 1，2，3，4 の中から一つ選び，その番号を解答用紙の所定欄にマークしなさい。

[A]

Sally's Concert

Sally has been taking piano lessons for about a year. She started because she heard her uncle Kevin playing when she visited his house. She thought that his music sounded wonderful. Sally has been practicing hard and learning quickly. Her teacher told her that there would be a concert for the students at the piano school and that Sally should take part. Sally (**26**), though. She thought that performing in public would be scary. However, her teacher said that it would be a good experience.

At the concert, Sally's parents and Uncle Kevin were in the audience. When it was time for Sally to play, she was worrying a lot. Her teacher told her to relax and enjoy the chance to (**27**). Sally did her best. When she finished playing, all the people in the audience were smiling, clapping, and cheering. This made Sally feel very special, and she knew that her teacher had been right.

(26) **1** could not see anything   **2** had to ask her parents

      3 did not have much money   **4** was very nervous

(27) **1** visit foreign countries   **2** make other people happy

      3 listen to famous pianists   **4** help sick children

[B]

Up and Away

Cars that can fly have appeared in many science-fiction stories. For over 100 years, people have been trying to build real flying cars. Some have succeeded, but their flying cars have never been produced in large numbers. These cars were usually too expensive for people to buy. However, a company in the European country of Slovakia thinks that its flying cars can be made (28   ). As a result, it might soon be common to see flying cars in the sky.

Stefan Klein, the owner of the company, has spent about 30 years trying to develop a flying car. In June 2021, Klein's car (29   ). It took 35 minutes to travel about 90 kilometers from the airport in Nitra to the one in Bratislava. After it landed, the flying car's wings were folded up in less than three minutes, and Klein drove the car to the city center. The car has now been flown over 200 times, and the government of Slovakia has decided to allow people to use it for air travel.

Klein thinks that his company will be able to sell many flying cars. He still faces several challenges, though. First, his flying car can only take off and land at airports. Also, it uses gasoline, so some people say that it is not good for the environment. (30   ), people need a pilot's license if they want to use the flying car. However, Klein thinks he will be able to solve these problems sometime soon.

(28) 1 at lower prices   2 in a shorter time

        3 from recycled paper   4 by a new kind of robot

(29) 1 went on sale   2 was hit by a truck

        3 made its first trip   4 won a famous race

(30) 1 Even so   2 Therefore

        3 Moreover   4 For example

23
年度第1回

筆記

4

次の英文 [A], [B] の内容に関して，(31) から (37) までの質問に対して最も適切なもの，または文を完成させるのに最も適切なものを 1, 2, 3, 4 の中から一つ選び，その番号を解答用紙の所定欄にマークしなさい。

[A]

From: Ralph Parker <ralph_parker@epostal.com>
To: Gary Jones <gazjones_101@mymessage.com>
Date: June 4
Subject: My cousins

Hi Gary,

We haven't had a chance to meet since you and your family moved to your new house. Are you enjoying your new school? I know there's a great park near your new place. My mom and dad took me there once after we went to the mall on that side of the city. I really wanted to try the basketball court there, but I didn't have my ball. Have you played on it yet?

By the way, do you remember my cousins from Seattle? We had fun with them when they visited last summer. They're coming to stay with us again at the end of this month. Would you like to come over while they're here? We could have a game of basketball with them. I've also got a new board game, and I think we would have a great time playing it.

My cousins will be staying with us from June 21 to June 29. They will also visit their other relatives in the city, so they'll be quite busy. Can you tell me a couple of dates when you can come? My dad says that if your mom or dad can bring you here, he will take you home in the evening. Please speak to your parents and let me know.

Your friend,
Ralph

(31) What is one thing that Ralph asks Gary?

   1 If Gary has tried the basketball court in his local park.
   2 If Gary bought a new basketball when he went to the mall.
   3 Whether Gary's new school is near his new house.
   4 Whether Gary's parents are planning to move to a new house.

(32) Ralph says that his cousins from Seattle

   1 will play in a basketball tournament in June.
   2 have told him about a great new board game.
   3 want to know if Gary can remember them.
   4 came to stay with his family last year.

(33) What does Ralph's father say that he will do?

   1 Speak to Gary's parents.
   2 Tell Ralph the best dates to come.
   3 Take Gary back to his house.
   4 Visit Ralph's relatives in the city.

[B]
Video Game Arcades

The first computer games were quite different from the ones that people play today. When computer games appeared in the 1950s, computers were big and expensive. They were only found in universities and large companies. Although computers were invented to solve serious problems, creating games is a good way to learn computer programming. In addition, the process of inventing new games has led to many important discoveries for computer technology.

In the early 1970s, computers were still too expensive for most people to own. However, a number of fun games had been developed by students at universities in the United States. Some of these students wanted to make money from their games. They built computers inside large wooden boxes. Then, they put the boxes in places like bars and cafés. Customers could play the games by putting money into a special hole in the boxes.

These computer games were a big success. More and more of them were created. One of the most popular games was *Space Invaders*. In this game, players tried to shoot space monsters that were attacking them. In the 1970s, "video game arcades" began to appear. These were places with many computer game machines. During the 1970s and 1980s, video game arcades became important places for young people to meet friends and make new ones.

At the same time, companies were developing cheap home computers. People with these machines did not have to go to video game arcades. They did not have to pay each time they wanted to play a game. They did not have to wait for other people to finish playing, either. Video game arcade owners tried to introduce games that used technology that home computers did not have. However, home computer makers were able to find ways to make their games more attractive. Now, many video game arcades have closed.

(34) Computer games can be used to

    1 train new staff members when they join large companies.
    2 help people understand how to make computer software.
    3 solve serious problems all over the world.
    4 find ways for universities to save money.

(35) Why did some students put computers in places like bars and cafés?

    1 To discover how much money people would pay for a computer.
    2 To do research on why computer games had become so popular.
    3 So that they could find out what food and drinks customers bought.
    4 So that they could get some money from the games they had made.

(36) One reason many young people went to "video game arcades" was

    1 that they could get to know new people.
    2 that they thought space monsters might attack.
    3 to show people the games they had created.
    4 to get jobs making computer game machines.

(37) How did owners try to get more people to come to their video game arcades?

    1 By introducing games that people could play without paying.
    2 By giving discounts on home computers to their best customers.
    3 By adding things for people to do while waiting to play games.
    4 By bringing in computer technology that people did not have at home.

5
- ●あなたは，外国人の知り合いから以下の QUESTION をされました。
- ● QUESTION について，あなたの意見とその理由を 2 つ英文で書きなさい。
- ●語数の目安は 50 語〜60 語です。
- ●解答は，解答用紙の B 面にあるライティング解答欄に書きなさい。なお，解答欄の外に書かれたものは採点されません。
- ●解答が QUESTION に対応していないと判断された場合は，0 点と採点されることがあります。 QUESTION をよく読んでから答えてください。

QUESTION
Do you think hospitals should be open on weekends?

（リスニングテストは次のページにあります。）

リスニング

準2級リスニングテストについて

1　このリスニングテストには，第1部から第3部まであります。
☆英文はすべて一度しか読まれません。
第1部：対話を聞き，その最後の文に対する応答として最も適切なものを，放送される
1，2，3の中から一つ選びなさい。
第2部：対話を聞き，その質問に対して最も適切なものを1，2，3，4の中から一つ選
びなさい。
第3部：英文を聞き，その質問に対して最も適切なものを1，2，3，4の中から一つ選
びなさい。
2　No. 30のあと，10秒すると試験終了の合図がありますので，筆記用具を置いてください。

||||||| 第1部 |||||||||||||||||||||||||||　◀)) ▶MP3 ▶アプリ ▶CD 1 43～53

No. 1～No. 10（選択肢はすべて放送されます。）

||||||| 第2部 |||||||||||||||||||||||||||　◀)) ▶MP3 ▶アプリ ▶CD 1 54～64

| No. 11 | 1 Read a newspaper.
2 Borrow some books.
3 Copy some magazine articles.
4 Fix the copy machine. |

| No. 12 | 1 Take a vacation overseas.
2 Go on a business trip.
3 Visit the man's mother.
4 Cancel their barbecue. |

| No. 13 | 1 The store will be having a sale soon.
2 The store will be closing in a few minutes.
3 The store does not have any wool sweaters.
4 The store does not have a light-blue skirt. |

No. 14	1 Take a drive.
	2 Bake a cake.
	3 Go to the supermarket.
	4 Look for his car key.

No. 15	1 His garage door was broken.
	2 His garage door needed to be painted.
	3 He wanted to repair her door.
	4 He had to cancel an appointment.

No. 16	1 She gave him a new guidebook.
	2 She bought his plane ticket online.
	3 She packed his suitcase for his trip.
	4 She reminded him to do something.

No. 17	1 See a game on TV with Jiro.
	2 Play baseball with Jiro.
	3 Go to Jiro's house.
	4 Watch Jiro's game.

No. 18	1 She went to the store after closing time.
	2 She broke her computer keyboard.
	3 The store does not have the red keyboard.
	4 The store does not sell computers.

No. 19	1 Go to a music concert.
	2 Have a business meeting.
	3 Visit another town.
	4 Play music together.

No. 20	1 He did not bring his hiking boots.
	2 He did not check the weather report.
	3 He went to the wrong mountain.
	4 He lost his brother's raincoat.

No. 21
1 To keep his food away from bears.
2 To buy food at the park's café.
3 To take pictures of the bears.
4 To call him before leaving the park.

No. 22
1 Take piano lessons.
2 Take swimming lessons.
3 Take judo lessons.
4 Take computer lessons.

No. 23
1 An important player got hurt.
2 The weather was bad.
3 The stadium was being repaired.
4 Only a few tickets could be sold.

No. 24
1 He played rugby on his school's team.
2 He played soccer on his father's team.
3 He went to soccer matches with his mother.
4 He went to a school with a famous rugby coach.

No. 25
1 He did not have enough cash.
2 He could not use his smartphone.
3 It was not open yet.
4 It did not have pasta.

No. 26
1 Her friend picked her up there.
2 Her friend worked there.
3 She wanted to buy a dress.
4 She needed new shoes.

No. 27
1 They can be used inside busy cities.
2 They can be driven easily at night.
3 Electric cars are difficult to charge outside of cities.
4 Electric cars are not allowed in some places.

No. 28	1 The parking lot is full.
	2 The mall is under construction.
	3 The store is closing soon.
	4 The sale will end tomorrow.

No. 29	1 There is a problem with the seat belts.
	2 There is a lot of snow outside.
	3 The airplane needs to be checked.
	4 The baggage arrived late.

No. 30	1 They are mainly active at night.
	2 They have very large heads.
	3 They dry their food in the sun.
	4 They dig holes under trees.

問題カード（A日程）　　🔊　▶MP3　▶アプリ　▶CD 1 76～80

Outdoor Activities

Outdoor activities are popular with people of all ages. For example, camping in nature is fun, and many people enjoy cooking outdoors. However, some people do not pay enough attention to others around them, and as a result they cause problems for other campers. People should think about others when enjoying outdoor activities.

A

B

Questions

No. 1   According to the passage, why do some people cause problems for other campers?

No. 2   Now, please look at the people in Picture A. They are doing different things. Tell me as much as you can about what they are doing.

No. 3   Now, look at the girl in Picture B. Please describe the situation.

Now, Mr. / Ms. _____, please turn over the card and put it down.

No. 4   Do you think that more people will go to cooking schools in the future?
Yes. → Why?
No. → Why not?

No. 5   In Japan, many kinds of tea are sold in stores. Do you often drink tea?
Yes. → Please tell me more.
No. → Why not?

Better Beaches

Today, beaches are popular with people of all ages. However, keeping beaches in good condition is hard work. Now, technology is playing an important role. Some towns use robots that clean beaches, and in this way they try to make the environment of their beaches better. Such robots are becoming more common.

A

B

Questions

No. 1   According to the passage, how do some towns try to make the environment of their beaches better?

No. 2   Now, please look at the people in Picture A. They are doing different things. Tell me as much as you can about what they are doing.

No. 3   Now, look at the girl in Picture B. Please describe the situation.

Now, Mr. / Ms. _____, please turn over the card and put it down.

No. 4   Do you think more people will want to have robots as pets in the future?
Yes. → Why?
No. → Why not?

No. 5   These days, going shopping with friends is popular among young people. Do you often go shopping with your friends?
Yes. → Please tell me more.
No. → Why not?

2022-3

一次試験 2023.1.22実施
二次試験 A日程 2023.2.19実施
　　　　 B日程 2023.2.26実施

Grade Pre-2

Pre 2

試験時間

筆記：75分
リスニング：約25分

＊解答・解説は別冊p.77〜112にあります。
＊面接の流れは本書p.24にあります。

1 次の (1) から (20) までの（　　　）に入れるのに最も適切なものを **1, 2, 3, 4** の中から一つ選び，その番号を解答用紙の所定欄にマークしなさい。

(1) The lifeguard at the hotel pool told the swimmers not to (　　　) there because the pool was not deep enough.
1 flow　　　　**2** melt　　　　**3** dive　　　　**4** announce

(2) Greg is going to play in a tennis tournament next weekend. He has only been playing for three months, so he is very (　　　) to win.
1 unlikely　　　**2** traditional　　**3** similar　　　**4** honest

(3) Jenny's dream is to become a famous writer. She wants to be like her favorite (　　　), who has written over 10 best-selling novels.
1 astronaut　　**2** accountant　　**3** author　　　**4** athlete

(4) When the dog took Linda's hat, Linda had to (　　　) it around the park to get it back.
1 chase　　　　**2** greet　　　　**3** hire　　　　**4** share

(5) It is easy to get around in big cities, such as Osaka and Fukuoka, because they have (　　　) of trains and buses.
1 struggles　　**2** recordings　　**3** networks　　**4** purposes

(6) The teacher (　　　) the class into small groups so they could discuss ideas for their projects.
1 accepted　　**2** warmed　　　**3** divided　　　**4** injured

(7) Sayaka and her father have very different opinions on (　　　) such as taxes and the environment.
1 degrees　　　**2** partners　　　**3** responses　　**4** issues

(8) Austin was sad after his girlfriend left him. However, he quickly forgot about her, and now he is in good (　　　) again.
1 contests　　　**2** spirits　　　**3** arguments　　**4** decisions

(9) *A:* Is it difficult to grow these flowers?
B: Not at all. You (   ) plant the seeds in the ground and make sure they get plenty of water.
1 loudly   **2** simply   **3** shortly   **4** finally

(10) Carl was very sorry for breaking his neighbor's window with his baseball. He went to his neighbor's house to (   ). He also promised to be more careful.
1 apologize   **2** export   **3** limit   **4** nod

(11) *A:* Ashley, which dress should I buy?
B: I don't know. They (   ) to me. They have the same buttons and they're both blue.
1 look ahead   **2** look alike   **3** catch on   **4** catch up

(12) Michael had to (   ) the campfire before he went to sleep in the tent. He went to the river to get some water and threw it on the fire.
1 come out   **2** put out   **3** fill up   **4** back up

(13) There are various ways to help people (   ). For example, you can give money, clothes, or food to people who do not have enough.
1 on end   **2** by heart   **3** in need   **4** of use

(14) Tony got a job as a train driver after he finished high school. He (   ) the railway company for almost 50 years. He left when he became 65 years old.
1 came over   **2** took after   **3** brought up   **4** worked for

(15) *A:* How long have you been (   )?
B: I started two months ago. So far, I've lost about 5 kilograms.
1 for a change   **2** on a diet   **3** in place   **4** with time

(16) Some types of birds are (   ) travel long distances. For example, arctic terns make journeys of around 90,000 kilometers each year.
1 jealous of   **2** belonged to   **3** known to   **4** true of

(17) Kelly loves the sea, but she has always lived far away from it. Her dream is to move to a house (   ) the ocean after she retires.

    1 certain of   **2** fit for   **3** close to   **4** poor at

(18) (   ) three months, a big market is held in Coopersville. The last one was held in December, so the next one will be held in March.

    1 All   **2** Every   **3** With   **4** Some

(19) Billy often listens to a radio channel called Sonic FM because he wants to hear the (   ) music. Sonic FM usually only plays songs from the past two or three months.

    1 highest   **2** latest   **3** fastest   **4** earliest

(20) Kenny gets angry when his parents tell him to go to bed or to eat his vegetables. He hates (   ) like a little child.

    1 treated   **2** being treated   **3** treating   **4** to be treating

次の四つの会話文を完成させるために，(21) から (25) に入るものとして最も適切なものを 1, 2, 3, 4 の中から一つ選び，その番号を解答用紙の所定欄にマークしなさい。

(21) *A:* Good evening, sir. Are you ready to order yet?

B: Do you still serve seafood pasta?

A: We used to, but we (**21**) recently.

B: That's a shame. I really liked that dish.

1 started opening later

2 got some new staff

3 bought some new chairs

4 changed our menu

---

(22) *A:* Dad, can you help me with my science homework?

B: Sure, Claire. What do you need to do?

A: I have to (**22**). Then, I have to color it and write the names of the different parts on it.

B: That sounds like fun. Let's go and choose one from the garden.

1 draw a picture of a plant

2 answer questions in my textbook

3 get some information about space

4 measure the size of my head

---

(23) *A:* What kind of clothes are you looking for, sir?

B: I heard about your sale. Can (**23**) if I bring you my old one?

A: Yes. However, today is the last chance to get that discount.

B: Right. I'll be back soon!

1 you give me 25 percent off a new car

2 you print a new receipt for me

3 I buy a new suit for half price

4 I get a new TV for less money

A: Mom, can my friend Jan come and stay at our house this weekend?

B: Hmm. I'm not sure. Won't you both have (**24**   )?

A: Our teacher said that after the tests this week, we wouldn't have to study this weekend.

B: I see. How about your room? Have you cleaned it?

A: Not yet, but I promise that I'll do it on Thursday evening.

B: OK, then. I'd better speak to Jan's mother first to make sure that it's OK for Jan to stay with us.

A: Thanks, Mom. I'll ask Jan to send me (**25**   ).

B: Actually, I think I already have it. Let me check my address book.

(24) 1 meetings to go to
     2 homework to do
     3 club activities
     4 doctor's appointments

(25) 1 her mom's phone number
     2 her grandma's cookie recipe
     3 a book for our tests
     4 a photo of her family

（筆記試験の問題は次のページに続きます。）

3 次の英文 [A], [B] を読み，その文意にそって (26) から (30) までの (　　　) に入れるのに最も適切なものを 1, 2, 3, 4 の中から一つ選び，その番号を解答用紙の所定欄にマークしなさい。

[A]

The Costume Party

　　The other day, Ryan invited Heather to his birthday party. Ryan said it was a costume party. He asked Heather to dress as her favorite cartoon character. Heather's favorite character is a witch who rides a broom* and delivers mail. She wears a blue dress and a red ribbon in her hair. Heather did not have a blue dress, but her mom had some blue cloth. She told Heather (　26　) instead. Heather helped her mother, and soon, she had a dress exactly like the one the witch wears.

　　On the day of Ryan's party, Heather remembered that she also needed a broom. She asked her mother, but her mother said that she did not have one. Then, Heather remembered seeing her neighbor, Mr. Jones, using one to sweep his yard. Heather ran to Mr. Jones's house to ask if she could (　27　). Luckily, Mr. Jones said yes. Heather was very happy because her costume was complete.

*broom: ほうき

(26) **1** that she should stay home

　　　2 that they could make one

　　　3 to wear a green one

　　　4 to choose another character

(27) **1** borrow it

　　　2 hide there

　　　3 help him

　　　4 get her ball

80

[B]

Escher's Amazing Art

Maurits Cornelis Escher was born in the Netherlands in 1898. After leaving high school, he went to college to study how to design buildings. However, he soon realized that he was not (**28**). In fact, he liked designing things that could not be built. He decided to study graphic art instead. A graphic artist is an artist who uses imagination, math, and tools like rulers to produce pictures.

After Escher graduated, he traveled for a long time in Italy. He really liked the countryside and the old buildings there. He often drew the places that he saw there in his pictures. He also visited Spain. There, he went to a castle where the walls were covered with interesting patterns. They gave him ideas for his own patterns, and he would sometimes use the shapes of animals in these designs. His experiences (**29**) had a very big effect on his art.

Escher's pictures often show things that are impossible in real life. In the picture *Ascending and Descending*, people are climbing stairs that return to the place where they started. In *Drawing Hands*, two hands are holding pencils and drawing each other. Escher's unusual art is (**30**). For example, about 200,000 visitors went to see an exhibition of his work in Tokyo in 2018. People in many countries like his pictures because they are beautiful and they make people think.

(28) **1** a creative person   **2** a clever teacher

       3 interested in construction   **4** good at drawing

(29) **1** in these two countries

       2 from his early childhood

       3 of working with his father

       4 while learning new languages

(30) **1** all kept in one place

       2 popular around the world

       3 not for sale anymore

       4 not nice to look at

4

[A]

From: Ariana Smith <arianaariana@peacemail.com>
To: Jane Jones <jane_j30101@thismail.com>
Date: January 22
Subject: Cooking club recipes

- -

Dear Jane,

I really enjoy our weekly cooking club meetings at the community center. All the members are so friendly. It's nice that the members take turns teaching each other recipes. I get nervous when it's my turn to teach, but I'm always happy afterward. Also, I've learned how to make a really wide variety of dishes this way. It's much better than having just one cooking teacher.

I was telling my friend David about our meetings. David works as a photographer and designer for a company that publishes books. He suggested that the cooking club members make a book of our favorite recipes. He said that he would help us to do it. We could make something to remember our meetings. A book of recipes would also be a great gift for friends and family members.

I really like his idea. What do you think? We could ask each of the members to prepare recipes for a snack, a salad, a soup, a main dish, and a dessert. We can then choose the ones that sound the best and make them during our meetings. David said that he would be happy to come and take pictures of our food. He'd like to try some of it, too!

Your friend,
Ariana

(31) What does Ariana say about the cooking club meetings?

    1 She thinks their cooking teacher is very friendly.
    2 She likes the way that members teach each other.
    3 She feels nervous when new members join.
    4 She wants them to be moved to a community center.

(32) What has Ariana's friend David suggested?

    1 Food made at cooking club meetings could be sold.
    2 Friends should be allowed to watch cooking club meetings.
    3 The members of the cooking club should produce a book.
    4 Ariana could get a job at his publishing company.

(33) David has offered to

    1 think of new recipes for the cooking club.
    2 choose the best dishes in a cooking competition.
    3 teach Ariana and Jane how to cook various dishes.
    4 take photos of food for the cooking club.

[B]
A Slow Life in the Trees

A sloth is a kind of animal that lives in the jungles of Central and South America. Sloths look like monkeys and spend most of their time up in the branches of trees. However, unlike monkeys, sloths live alone, move very slowly, and make almost no noise. They sleep for up to 20 hours each day and only wake up during the night.

Sloths' lazy lifestyles help them to survive. By sleeping most of the time and moving slowly, sloths do not have to use much energy. They do not have to travel long distances or run fast to get something to eat. High up in the trees, a tasty leaf is always just a few centimeters away. Even though leaves do not contain many calories, sloths get all they need by eating all the time during the short time that they are awake.

Surprisingly, moving slowly also protects sloths from hungry meat eaters. Eagles and big cats live in the same jungles as sloths. However, these hunters search for movement, so they often do not notice sloths. Also, sloths do not clean their fur completely. As a result, tiny plants grow in it, and these make the fur look green. From the ground or the sky, a sloth in a tree's branches looks like a plant rather than something that an eagle or a big cat wants to eat.

Sloths have long, hard claws on their toes. Usually, they use their claws to hang on to branches. However, if a sloth is attacked, it can use its claws to defend itself. Sloths' claws are so long that sloths find it difficult to walk on the ground. Because of this, a sloth usually only comes down from the branches about once a week.

(34) What is one way sloths are different from monkeys?

    1 Sloths can be found in North America.
    2 Sloths often make a lot of noise.
    3 Sloths usually live by themselves.
    4 Sloths are only awake during the day.

(35) What is one reason that sloths move slowly?

    1 To reduce the amount of energy that they use.
    2 To allow them to travel very long distances.
    3 To catch the things that they like to eat.
    4 To avoid falling into holes made by other animals.

(36) Eagles and big cats

    1 do not eat sloths because their fur tastes bad.
    2 eat plants if they are not able to find meat.
    3 hunt by looking for the movement of animals.
    4 stay away from the jungles where sloths live.

(37) A sloth uses its long claws to

    1 cut open fruits that grow in the trees.
    2 get insects that live inside wood.
    3 jump from one tree to another.
    4 help it to hold on to branches.

5
- ●あなたは，外国人の知り合いから以下の **QUESTION** をされました。
- ● **QUESTION** について，あなたの意見とその<u>理由を 2 つ</u>英文で書きなさい。
- ●語数の目安は **50 語～60 語**です。
- ●解答は，解答用紙の **B** 面にあるライティング解答欄に書きなさい。<u>なお，解答欄の外に書かれたものは採点されません。</u>
- ●解答が **QUESTION** に対応していないと判断された場合は，<u>**0** 点と採点されることがあります。</u> **QUESTION** をよく読んでから答えてください。

QUESTION
Do you think libraries should have more book events for children?

（リスニングテストは次のページにあります。）

リスニング

準2級リスニングテストについて

1　このリスニングテストには，第1部から第3部まであります。
　☆英文はすべて一度しか読まれません。
　第1部：対話を聞き，その最後の文に対する応答として最も適切なものを，放送される
　　　　 1，2，3の中から一つ選びなさい。
　第2部：対話を聞き，その質問に対して最も適切なものを1，2，3，4の中から一つ選
　　　　 びなさい。
　第3部：英文を聞き，その質問に対して最も適切なものを1，2，3，4の中から一つ選
　　　　 びなさい。
2　No.30のあと，10秒すると試験終了の合図がありますので，筆記用具を置いてください。

|||||| 第1部 |||||| 🔊 ▶MP3 ▶アプリ ▶CD 2 **1**～**11**

No. 1～No. 10（選択肢はすべて放送されます。）

|||||| 第2部 |||||| 🔊 ▶MP3 ▶アプリ ▶CD 2 **12**～**22**

No. 11
1 It has a new dolphin.
2 It has few animals.
3 It will have a special show.
4 It will be closing next week.

No. 12
1 Heat up her plate.
2 Give her some more pasta.
3 Tell her about a new dish.
4 Bring her the check.

No. 13
1 She could not leave the hotel.
2 She did not go to any museums.
3 She went on a sightseeing tour.
4 She stayed outside of the city.

No. 14	1 He wants a salad with his sandwich.
	2 He needs to leave the restaurant soon.
	3 He is ordering for a friend.
	4 He feels very hungry today.

No. 15	1 Visit her grandma's house.
	2 Go to a wedding in the mountains.
	3 Plan a trip to a lake with the boy.
	4 Play table tennis with her aunt.

No. 16	1 Take his son to a class.
	2 Make some chicken soup.
	3 Clean the refrigerator.
	4 Take out the garbage.

No. 17	1 He has to return some clothes.
	2 He needs some new shoes.
	3 He has to buy a present.
	4 He heard about a sale.

No. 18	1 Get a new music CD.
	2 Have a party at home.
	3 Play in a concert.
	4 Go to a rock concert.

No. 19	1 She wanted to rent the space.
	2 She did not have time to get coffee.
	3 She liked to study at the coffee shop.
	4 She could not find the newspaper.

No. 20	1 To ask about the restaurant's menu.
	2 To get directions to the restaurant.
	3 To make a reservation for dinner.
	4 To order some special food items.

No. 21
1 Study to be a teacher.
2 Become an artist.
3 Make her own brushes.
4 Win a prize in a contest.

No. 22
1 To keep people caught by the police.
2 To make musical instruments.
3 To plan important events.
4 To design fashion items.

No. 23
1 The one for ice cream.
2 The one for vegetable soup.
3 The one for meat stew.
4 The one for chocolate cake.

No. 24
1 An offer is only available for one day.
2 The store will close soon.
3 All goods are only $20 today.
4 Only a few soap and shampoo products are left.

No. 25
1 Finding an interesting topic.
2 Asking her brother about science.
3 Giving a presentation to her class.
4 Going to school by herself.

No. 26
1 How to use a smartphone.
2 Choosing fashionable clothes.
3 Interesting places in her town.
4 Her favorite actors and directors.

No. 27
1 People can only eat them if they are cooked.
2 Romans were the first people to eat them.
3 Scotland produces more than any other country.
4 They are able to grow well in cold areas.

No. 28

1 The tickets were sold out.
2 The concert was canceled.
3 Amy did not want to go with him.
4 Amy does not like baseball.

No. 29

1 To explain how to buy tickets.
2 To tell passengers about a new bus stop.
3 The bus station will close soon.
4 A bus has been delayed.

No. 30

1 See a doctor about his arm.
2 Watch his team's basketball game.
3 Ride his bicycle with his friends.
4 Practice passing the ball.

問題カード（A日程）　　◀⟩ ▶MP3 ▶アプリ ▶CD 2 34～38

Keeping the Air Clean

Today, air cleaners play important roles in places such as hospitals and schools. However, air cleaners can be very big and difficult to put in every room. Now, some companies are making smaller types of air cleaners, and by doing so they help more places to keep the air clean.

A

B

Questions

No. 1   According to the passage, how do some companies help more places to keep the air clean?

No. 2   Now, please look at the people in Picture A. They are doing different things. Tell me as much as you can about what they are doing.

No. 3   Now, look at the man in Picture B. Please describe the situation.

Now, Mr. / Ms. _____, please turn over the card and put it down.

No. 4   Do you think students today have enough time to relax?
Yes. → Why?
No. → Why not?

No. 5   These days, many people enjoy buying and selling things at flea markets. Do you often go to flea markets to buy things?
Yes. → Please tell me more.
No. → Why not?

Staying Open All Night

In Japan, there are many stores that are open all day and night. However, some stores worry about the cost of staying open 24 hours, so they choose to close at night. Some customers do not think this is convenient, but more stores will probably stop staying open all night.

A

B

Questions

No. 1 According to the passage, why do some stores choose to close at night?

No. 2 Now, please look at the people in Picture A. They are doing different things. Tell me as much as you can about what they are doing.

No. 3 Now, look at the man and his daughter in Picture B. Please describe the situation.

Now, Mr. / Ms. ＿＿, please turn over the card and put it down.

No. 4 Do you think it is a good idea for schools to have cafeterias for their students?
Yes. → Why?
No. → Why not?

No. 5 In Japan, many festivals are held in different seasons. Do you often go to festivals in your town?
Yes. → Please tell me more.
No. → Why not?

2022-2

一次試験 2022.10.9実施
二次試験 Ａ日程 2022.11. 6 実施
　　　　 Ｂ日程 2022.11.13実施

Grade Pre-2

試験時間

筆記：75分
リスニング：約25分

＊解答・解説は別冊p.113〜148にあります。
＊面接の流れは本書p.24にあります。

1 次の **(1)** から **(20)** までの（　　　）に入れるのに最も適切なものを **1, 2, 3, 4** の中から一つ選び，その番号を解答用紙の所定欄にマークしなさい。

(1) The two leaders decided to stop the war between their countries. They promised their people that there would be (　　　).
1 peace　　　**2** faith　　　**3** honor　　　**4** matter

(2) Troy's feet have grown so much this year that none of his shoes (　　　) him. His mother is taking him shopping today to buy new ones.
1 sew　　　**2** fit　　　**3** cure　　　**4** gain

(3) The little girl wanted to play with the cat. But whenever she (　　　) it, the cat ran away.
1 celebrated　**2** approached　**3** separated　**4** researched

(4) Momoko lives in Tokyo, which is in the (　　　) part of Japan. Every summer, she takes a train and visits her grandfather in Osaka, which is in the west.
1 relative　　**2** eastern　　**3** smooth　　**4** brave

(5) Xiang could not go to work for two weeks because of a serious (　　　). She had to take a lot of medicine and went to see the doctor many times.
1 illness　　**2** facility　　**3** decade　　**4** immigration

(6) Before Yasuko moved to her new apartment in Tokyo, she bought some (　　　). However, when she moved in, there was not enough space for the table and the bed.
1 atmosphere　**2** religion　　**3** furniture　　**4** poverty

(7) In recent years, the city has had to build many new roads and schools because its population has grown so (　　　).
1 exactly　　**2** pleasantly　**3** fairly　　**4** rapidly

(8) Cars are safer than motorcycles, but the (　　　) of motorcycles is that they use less gasoline.

1 advantage　　　　　　　　**2** destruction
3 laboratory　　　　　　　　**4** concentration

(9) The colors on a map sometimes show different features of the earth. Blue is used to (　　　) water, and green is often used to show forests.

1 develop　　**2** exchange　　**3** represent　　**4** guide

(10) When my parents were young, a milkman brought milk to their homes every day, just like postmen and postwomen (　　　) letters to us now.

1 balance　　**2** deliver　　**3** operate　　**4** replace

(11) *A:* Brian, I think the new boy at school is really cute, but I don't know his name.
B: He's in my gym class. I'll find (　　　) his name for you.

1 out　　　　**2** up　　　　**3** above　　　**4** away

(12) *A:* I'm taking a drawing class, but my pictures are always terrible!
B: Just (　　　) trying. It takes a long time to learn a skill like that.

1 turn on　　**2** keep on　　**3** bring up　　**4** sit up

(13) Andrew applied (　　　) three jobs, and he is now waiting to hear if any of the companies want to interview him.

1 about　　**2** for　　　**3** by　　　**4** across

(14) Lisa speaks to her parents on the phone every week because she lives far away and she misses them. After she (　　　), she soon starts to miss them again.

1 hangs up　　**2** carries out　　**3** puts away　　**4** goes ahead

(15) Sharon is really scared of spiders. There was one in her bedroom the other day. She jumped (　　　) of it, screamed, and hid in the bathroom.

1 for the life　　**2** in the light　　**3** at the sight　　**4** on the point

(16) Mr. Simmons not only teaches his students to play the piano but also tells them in (   ) about the lives of the most famous pianists in history.

1 case   **2** detail   **3** hand   **4** touch

(17) Daisy tried to (   ) in several ways when she was at college. She had jobs in the college library and cafeteria, and she even worked as a model for art classes.

1 take pride   **2** make money
3 give birth   **4** lose speed

(18) Jane's sister has four sons. One is a high school student, and (   ) are elementary school students.

1 all another   **2** another ones
3 the other   **4** the others

(19) Sandra thought her pet dog Charlie looked so cute (   ) his new jacket. She took some photos of him and shared them online with her friends.

1 at   **2** in   **3** of   **4** behind

(20) Barcelona is the (   ) city in Spain. Only Madrid is bigger.

1 second-largest   **2** second-larger
3 two-larger   **4** two-largest

次の四つの会話文を完成させるために，(21) から (25) に入るものとして最も適切なものを 1，2，3，4 の中から一つ選び，その番号を解答用紙の所定欄にマークしなさい。

2

(21) *A:* Soccer practice normally finishes at 5 p.m., but Coach Stevens said that today's practice will finish at six.
　B: Really? Did he say that? I didn't hear him. I'd better call my mom and ask her to (　**21**　).
　A: Do you want to use my phone?
　B: Thanks! My mom will be angry if she has to wait for an hour.

　1 bring my soccer shoes
　2 pick me up later than usual
　3 speak to Coach Stevens
　4 keep my dinner warm

- -

(22) *A:* Excuse me. Could you help me to find a book about making a garden?
　B: Certainly. We have several books that can help you. Do you plan to (　**22**　)?
　A: Hmm. I think it would be fun to start with things I can eat, like potatoes and carrots.
　B: Then, this book will be perfect for you.

　1 do it with someone else
　2 buy more than one book
　3 come to the library often
　4 grow flowers or vegetables

- -

(23) *A:* Let's order some sausage pizzas for lunch after the meeting tomorrow. Four should be enough.
　B: Wait. Pete and Sarah don't eat meat.
　A: You're right. We'd better get something for them, too.
　B: Let's get (　**23**　).

　1 two sausage pizzas and two chicken pizzas
　2 four extra-large chicken pizzas
　3 one sausage pizza and one vegetarian pizza
　4 three sausage pizzas and one vegetarian pizza

A: Mr. Taylor, I don't know what topic to choose for the class presentation. Can you help me?

B: OK. Think about the things we've studied in class this year. Was there anything you liked?

A: Well, I really enjoyed learning about (**24**).

B: That would be a good topic. For example, you could talk about the strange fish that live deep in the sea.

A: That's a great idea! I think there's something about them in our textbook.

B: OK, but you should also (**25**).

A: I'll see what I can find at the library. Also, I can take a look on the Internet.

B: If you need more help, come and talk to me anytime.

(24) **1** life in the ocean
2 famous travelers
3 recycling metal
4 stars and planets

(25) **1** work with a partner
2 look for other information
3 practice your presentation
4 talk to your parents

（筆記試験の問題は次のページに続きます。）

3 次の英文 [A], [B] を読み，その文意にそって (26) から (30) までの (　　) に入れるのに最も適切なものを 1, 2, 3, 4 の中から一つ選び，その番号を解答用紙の所定欄にマークしなさい。

[A]

A Voice from the Past

Every year, volunteers in Brisbane, Australia, meet to clean up the beach. This year, John and his father joined the group. They worked hard all morning to pick up garbage. Near lunchtime, John noticed a glass bottle on the beach. The bottle was old and dirty. It looked like (**26**). John picked up the bottle and gave it to his father. His father opened it and took out a piece of paper. He told John that it was a message.

John's father showed the message to John. It said, "My name is Paul, and I am 10 years old. I am from Canada. I am traveling to Australia on a ship called the *Fair Star*. Please (**27**)." On their way home, John and his father bought a postcard to send to Paul. A few weeks later, they got a reply. Paul said he was now 50, and it was amazing that John had found his message after such a long time.

(26) **1** it had been made recently

    2 it was full of red wine

    3 there might be more bottles nearby

    4 there was something inside it

(27) **1** write to me at this address

    2 have a nice time on vacation

    3 take this bottle to my family

    4 help me to get back home

[B]

Hungry Hikers

People are having a bigger and bigger effect on wild animals. As a result, new laws and special parks are being created to protect nature. Some changes have been very successful. For example, there were about 170 wild elephants in 1980 in Yunnan, China. These days, experts think that there are around 300 elephants there. However, the elephants have (**28**). As cities get bigger and more farms are needed to feed people, there are not as many places for animals like elephants.

Big animals can cause big problems for people. Because there is not enough food in protected areas, elephants often leave these areas to take food from farms. In fact, a group of about 14 elephants from Yunnan went on a 500-kilometer walk to look for food during 2020 and 2021. The elephants sometimes went through towns trying to find food. They appeared on the TV news and the Internet. As a result, they (**29**) China. People were interested to find out what would happen to them next.

Finally, the elephants returned to a protected area in Yunnan. However, to try to prevent similar adventures in the future, experts have designed a special "food court" for elephants. The food court cost $15 million to build and is about 670,000 square meters. It has five ponds where elephants can drink, and all the plants that elephants need to eat to stay healthy. The experts hope that it will be enough to (**30**).

(28) 1 fewer chances to see people

     2 less space to live in

     3 shorter lives than before

     4 smaller numbers of babies

(29) 1 tried some food from   2 were kept in zoos outside

     3 decided to travel to   4 got a lot of attention in

(30) 1 attract more human visitors

     2 stop people from killing animals

     3 keep the elephants in the area

     4 make the elephants sleepy

[A]

From: Alan Reznick <alanreznick@bmail.com>
To: Jeff Teanaway <jeff.t@wmail.com>
Date: October 9
Subject: Movie festival

Hi Jeff,

Thanks for letting me borrow your DVD of *Burning Fist*. It's such an exciting movie. I really liked the part when the hero is riding a cool bike and being chased by bad guys. After watching it last Saturday, my mom took me to a bookstore. I found a book about *Burning Fist* and bought it. It's really interesting. I'll lend it to you when I finish reading it.

While I was at the bookstore, I saw a poster for an action movie festival. It will be held next month at the Old Lawrence Theater, near the Elm Street subway station. It's close to the Mexican restaurant that we went to on your birthday last year. The poster said that the director of *Burning Fist* will be at the festival. She'll answer fans' questions about her movies and talk about her next movie.

Eight movies are going to be shown over two days at the festival. They've all been chosen by the director of *Burning Fist*. Some of them are old action movies from the 1980s and 1990s. There will also be some new movies, too. I think it sounds great, so I'm definitely going to buy a ticket for the festival. Should I get one for you, too?

Talk soon,
Alan

(31) What did Alan do last Saturday?

    1 He went to a bookstore with Jeff.
    2 He bought a book about a movie.
    3 He rode a friend's cool bike.
    4 He lent one of his DVDs to Jeff.

(32) Last year, Jeff and Alan

    1 tried Mexican food for the first time.
    2 watched a movie at the Old Lawrence Theater.
    3 met the director of *Burning Fist*.
    4 went to a restaurant for Jeff's birthday.

(33) What is one thing Alan says about the festival?

    1 He has already bought tickets for it.
    2 All the movies are old action movies.
    3 The movies were chosen by local movie fans.
    4 It will be held on more than one day.

[B]

Spicy Soda

Ginger ale is a spicy soft drink. It was invented in Ireland in the 1850s. However, the type that is most popular today was created by a man called John McLaughlin who lived in Toronto, Canada. After he graduated from college in Canada, he went to study in New York City. While studying, he worked part-time at a drugstore. He noticed that many people were buying soda water from the store and mixing it with different fruit flavors.

McLaughlin returned to Toronto in 1890 and started a soda water company. It became very successful. One reason was that his advertisements said the water provided by the city was dangerous and caused diseases. He recommended that people drink his fruit-flavored soda water instead. He also made machines called soda fountains. People could use them to buy McLaughlin's drinks. The machines became popular with shoppers in busy department stores, especially on hot summer days.

McLaughlin had poor health, and he had to stop being the manager of his company. However, he continued inventing new drinks. He knew about ginger ale from Ireland, but many of his customers did not like its sweet flavor. McLaughlin spent three years trying to create the perfect kind of ginger ale. Finally, by 1904, he had created a lighter, spicier drink. McLaughlin's wife liked it so much that she said it was "the champagne of ginger ales."

McLaughlin's "Canada Dry Pale Ginger Ale" was a success. As well as being delicious on its own, it could also be mixed with other drinks. Some people like to drink it rather than beer or other alcoholic drinks. Moreover, the ginger can help people with stomachaches or sore throats. It has been over 100 years since Canada Dry Pale Ginger Ale was invented. In that time, its popularity has spread from Canada, through the United States, and around the world.

(34) What did John McLaughlin notice while he was in New York City?

    1 People from Ireland liked to drink ginger ale.
    2 It was easier to find work there than in Canada.
    3 Adding different flavors to soda water was popular.
    4 Drugstores there sold more things than drugstores in Toronto.

(35) What is one reason that people bought McLaughlin's drinks?

    1 They heard that soda water could sometimes cause diseases.
    2 There was an unusually hot summer in the year 1890.
    3 McLaughlin told them that the water in Toronto was not safe.
    4 McLaughlin sold his drinks outside busy department stores.

(36) What was one result of McLaughlin's poor health?

    1 He quit his job as manager.
    2 He went on a trip to Ireland.
    3 He started eating more ginger.
    4 He stopped drinking champagne.

(37) Some people like to drink "Canada Dry Pale Ginger Ale"

    1 because other drinks give them stomachaches.
    2 instead of drinks such as beer or wine.
    3 when they go traveling in other countries.
    4 to stay awake when they have to work or study.

5

● あなたは，外国人の知り合いから以下の QUESTION をされました。

● QUESTION について，あなたの意見とその<u>理由を 2 つ</u>英文で書きなさい。

● 語数の目安は **50 語〜60 語**です。

● 解答は，解答用紙の **B** 面にあるライティング解答欄に書きなさい。<u>なお，解答欄の外に書かれたものは採点されません。</u>

● 解答が QUESTION に対応していないと判断された場合は，<u>0 点と採点されることがあります。</u> QUESTION をよく読んでから答えてください。

QUESTION

Do you think it is good for people to use smartphones while studying?

（リスニングテストは次のページにあります。）

リスニング

準2級リスニングテストについて

‖‖‖ **第1部** ‖‖‖‖‖‖‖‖‖‖‖‖‖‖‖‖ 🔊 ▶MP3 ▶アプリ ▶CD 2 **43**〜**53**

No. 1〜No. 10（選択肢はすべて放送されます。）

‖‖‖ **第2部** ‖‖‖‖‖‖‖‖‖‖‖‖‖‖‖‖ 🔊 ▶MP3 ▶アプリ ▶CD 2 **54**〜**64**

No. 11
1 A kind of pasta to buy.
2 A bakery on Third Street.
3 A place to go for dinner.
4 A supermarket downtown.

No. 12
1 Visit her sister.
2 Feed her neighbor's cat.
3 Stay home.
4 Go camping.

No. 13
1 Getting some money at a bank.
2 Shopping at a clothing store.
3 Talking to a clerk at a post office.
4 Booking a trip at a travel agency.

No. 14
1 There is salad for school lunch.
2 The cafeteria serves pizza.
3 Her mother makes burgers for dinner.
4 She has a cooking class.

No. 15
1 He did well on a math test.
2 He wants to take a piano lesson.
3 He found Karen's math book.
4 He will invite Karen to his house.

No. 16
1 By reading a cookbook.
2 By practicing for years.
3 By watching *Best Chefs*.
4 By learning from his grandmother.

No. 17
1 To keep students from talking.
2 To make his lessons interesting.
3 To help students with their homework.
4 To prepare students for traveling.

No. 18
1 Making a drink with lemons.
2 Cooking food at a barbecue.
3 Setting the dining table for lunch.
4 Making a list for the grocery store.

No. 19
1 He cannot find a good doctor.
2 He has a stomachache.
3 His medicine does not taste good.
4 His job is very stressful.

No. 20
1 Order a chocolate cake.
2 Sell cakes to Brenda.
3 Go to the bakery.
4 Make a cake himself.

No. 21
1 She had to walk for a long time.
2 She stayed up late watching TV.
3 Her train was very crowded.
4 Her office is far from her house.

No. 22
1 They drew pictures of nature together.
2 They went to catch fish together.
3 She took him to meet her family.
4 She visited him at a safari park.

No. 23
1 She used an old textbook.
2 She finished it late.
3 She copied her friend's answers.
4 She had done the wrong questions.

No. 24
1 A storm is coming later in the day.
2 A sports program is going to be canceled.
3 There were strong winds in the morning.
4 There will be an exciting movie in the evening.

No. 25
1 To eat lunch with her friends.
2 To run and do exercises.
3 To see her friend's dog.
4 To play with her new pet.

No. 26
1 She broke one of her ski poles.
2 She forgot her skis at home.
3 Her friends said it was cool.
4 Her family bought her some lessons.

No. 27
1 At special events.
2 When people felt sick.
3 In the middle of the morning.
4 When people wanted money.

No. 28	1 It was cheaper than the other toys.
	2 Its box was his favorite color.
	3 His parents had a similar one.
	4 There was a picture of a car on it.

No. 29	1 To walk his pet.
	2 To try breakdancing.
	3 To watch a performance.
	4 To help his sister practice.

No. 30	1 There was an accident at a station.
	2 There was a problem on the tracks.
	3 Its doors were not able to close.
	4 Its radio was not working well.

面　接

A New Way of Recycling

Today, supermarkets are trying to help the environment. They have started services that let customers recycle plastic more easily. Some customers take plastic bottles to supermarkets, and by doing so they get a discount for shopping there. Such supermarkets are trying to make the environment better and attract customers at the same time.

A

B

Questions

No. 1   According to the passage, how do some customers get a discount for shopping at supermarkets?

No. 2   Now, please look at the people in Picture A. They are doing different things. Tell me as much as you can about what they are doing.

No. 3   Now, look at the man in Picture B. Please describe the situation.

Now, Mr. / Ms. _____, please turn over the card and put it down.

No. 4   Do you think students should have more time to use computers at school?
Yes. → Why?
No. → Why not?

No. 5   In Japan, many people enjoy hiking in their free time. Do you like to go hiking?
Yes. → Please tell me more.
No. → Why not?

Audio Books

Today, many books that are read and recorded by professional actors are sold on the Internet. These books are called audio books. People can enjoy listening to audio books while doing other things, so they find these books very convenient. Audio books will probably become even more popular in the future.

A

B

Questions

No. 1   According to the passage, why do people find audio books very convenient?

No. 2   Now, please look at the people in Picture A. They are doing different things. Tell me as much as you can about what they are doing.

No. 3   Now, look at the man and the woman in Picture B. Please describe the situation.

Now, Mr. / Ms. _____, please turn over the card and put it down.

No. 4   Do you think watching the news on TV is better than reading newspapers?
Yes. → Why?
No. → Why not?

No. 5   These days, there are many books and magazines about cooking. Do you often cook at home?
Yes. → Please tell me more.
No. → Why not?

2022-1

一次試験 2022.6.5実施
二次試験 A日程 2022.7. 3 実施
　　　　 B日程 2022.7.10実施

Grade Pre-2

Pre

╺ 試験時間 ╸

筆記：75分
リスニング：約25分

＊解答・解説は別冊p.149〜184にあります。
＊面接の流れは本書p.24にあります。

1 次の (1) から (20) までの (　　　) に入れるのに最も適切なものを 1, 2, 3, 4 の中から一つ選び，その番号を解答用紙の所定欄にマークしなさい。

(1) Lisa read a (　　　) on the side of the road. It said to watch out for falling rocks.
1 warning　　**2** channel　　**3** shade　　**4** variety

(2) Tomoko wants her (　　　) with Yuji to continue even after they go to different junior high schools next year.
1 knowledge　**2** supply　　**3** friendship　**4** license

(3) Andrew was having trouble in Spanish class, so his teacher gave him some (　　　) homework. He learned a lot by spending more time making sentences in Spanish.
1 peaceful　　**2** talented　　**3** additional　**4** negative

(4) Michael's parents (　　　) him to become a teacher, but Michael wanted to be an artist. In the end, he became an art teacher.
1 celebrated　**2** filled　　　**3** pushed　　**4** escaped

(5) *A:* We've been driving for a long time, Dad. When will we get to Grandma's house?
B: It's not far now, Beth. We'll (　　　) her house in about 10 minutes.
1 measure　　**2** count　　　**3** reach　　**4** promise

(6) *A:* I can't believe Naomi Jones won the tennis championship this year!
B: Yes, it's a great (　　　), especially since she lost her first two matches of the season.
1 achievement　　　　　　**2** retirement
3 treatment　　　　　　　**4** equipment

(7) When Victoria started typing on the computer for the first time, she was very slow. However, she practiced every day and (　　　) became able to type very fast.
1 rarely　　**2** heavily　　**3** brightly　　**4** eventually

(8) At first, Bob felt nervous about performing a guitar solo in the school concert. But he found the (   ) to do it after talking to his guitar teacher.

1 courage   **2** fashion   **3** education   **4** average

(9) Melissa (   ) when she saw a mouse on the kitchen floor. Her husband ran to the kitchen to find out why she had made so much noise.

1 decorated   **2** harvested   **3** graduated   **4** screamed

(10) Clark's little brother likes to dress up in black clothes and (   ) to be a ninja.

1 expect   **2** explode   **3** pretend   **4** protest

(11) Jane trained every day for a marathon in summer. In the end, she (   ) finishing the race in fewer than four hours.

1 complained of   **2** came into
3 stood by   **4** succeeded in

(12) Mike looked when the tour guide pointed and said that there were elephants (   ). However, he could not see them because they were too far away.

1 on air   **2** as a rule
3 in the distance   **4** at most

(13) *A:* Why do you want to go on a date to the mall, Jenny? (   ) shopping, what else can we do there?
    B: Well, there are some great places to eat in the mall. There's a movie theater, too.

1 Aside from   **2** Compared with
3 Based on   **4** Close to

(14) Emma enjoyed sitting on the beach and watching the sun go down and the stars come out. (   ), it began to get cold, so she decided to go back to her hotel.

1 After a while   **2** In a word
3 For the best   **4** By the way

(15) Spencer does not like to (   ) when he uses his bicycle. He always wears his helmet and rides carefully.
1 make efforts   **2** make progress
3 take place   **4** take risks

(16) Bobby saw smoke coming out of his neighbor's kitchen window. He realized that his neighbor's house was (   ), so he went and told his mother right away.
1 with luck   **2** on fire   **3** at sea   **4** for sale

(17) *A:* I heard Randy dropped his cell phone in the river.
B: Yeah. He said it was an accident, but I think he did it (   ) because he wanted his parents to buy him a new one.
1 with help   **2** for free   **3** in place   **4** on purpose

(18) Jason's parents were in the drama club together during high school. That is (   ) they first got to know each other.
1 how   **2** what   **3** whose   **4** who

(19) Last night, Rick's mom would not let him (   ) TV until he had finished cleaning his room.
1 to watch   **2** watch   **3** watching   **4** watched

(20) *A:* Did you enjoy your trip to Bali?
B: Yes, very much. It's such a beautiful place, and the people there are very kind. It was worth (   ).
1 visit   **2** visiting   **3** to visit   **4** visited

次の四つの会話文を完成させるために，(21) から (25) に入るものとして最も適切なものを 1, 2, 3, 4 の中から一つ選び，その番号を解答用紙の所定欄にマークしなさい。

(21) **A:** Hello. My name is Peter Mason. I have (　**21**　).
　　　B: Please let me check, Mr. Mason. Yes, I see. We have a nonsmoking, double room for you. Is that OK?
　　　A: Yes. That will be fine.
　　　B: Thank you, sir. Here's your key. Your room is number 404, which is on the fourth floor.

　　1 a reservation for two nights
　　2 an appointment with the doctor
　　3 a meeting with Ms. Grant at four
　　4 a package to pick up

(22) **A:** Hi, Eric. Where's Mandy? I thought she would be with you.
　　　B: She called me earlier to say that (　**22**　) this evening.
　　　A: Oh. Did she say why?
　　　B: Yes. Her boss asked her to come to work because one of her co-workers is sick.

　　1 there'll be a full moon
　　2 it might rain
　　3 she can't come
　　4 her car won't start

(23) **A:** Welcome to Drawlish Tourist Information Center. How can I help you?
　　　B: (　**23**　) in Drawlish?
　　　A: I'm sorry, sir. There used to be one, but it closed several years ago.
　　　B: That's too bad. I think that watching fish swim can be very relaxing.

　　1 Are there any rivers
　　2 How many museums do you have
　　3 What's the best gift shop
　　4 Is there an aquarium

A: Dad, I made a sandwich earlier, but I don't see it anywhere. Do you know where it is?

B: Did it (**24**)?

A: Yes, it did. They're my favorite things to put in a sandwich.

B: Sorry! I thought your mother made it for me. I ate it just now for breakfast.

A: What? Oh no! I won't have anything to eat for lunch today.

B: Don't worry. I'll make you another one.

A: But the school bus will be here in three minutes.

B: It's OK. I'll (**25**) today.

(24) **1** have tuna and mayonnaise in it
2 come from the sandwich shop
3 take a long time to make
4 taste like strawberry jam

(25) **1** be at home all day
2 go to the supermarket
3 take you in my car
4 eat at a restaurant

（筆記試験の問題は次のページに続きます。）

次の英文 [A], [B] を読み，その文意にそって (26) から (30) までの (　　) に入れるのに最も適切なものを 1, 2, 3, 4 の中から一つ選び，その番号を解答用紙の所定欄にマークしなさい。

[A]

Good Friends

Hiroko and three of her friends have been working on a project for school. They have been doing research on the history of their town, and they must give a presentation about it in class next week. Every day after school, they have been getting together in the school library. They have been discussing what information to use and how to make a great presentation. They had some good ideas, and they were looking forward to (**26**).

However, Hiroko broke her leg during volleyball practice yesterday. Now, she must stay in the hospital for five days. She called her friends and said that she was sorry for not being able to do anything more to help them with the presentation. They told her not to worry. They said that their teacher is going to make a video of their presentation. That way, Hiroko will be able to (**27**). Hiroko thanked her friends and wished them good luck.

(26) **1** talking in front of their classmates

   2 making food for their teachers

   3 performing their musical in public

   4 seeing their book in bookstores

(27) **1** get well soon   **2** watch it afterwards

   3 take part as well   **4** play other sports

[B]
Getting to Know New Orleans

New Orleans is a city in the southern United States. In the past, people from France, Spain, Africa, and the Caribbean came to live there. As a result, it has a unique culture. This can be seen in the design of the city's buildings and heard in the city's music. Visitors can also experience this culture by (**28**) that come from New Orleans and the area around it. For example, visitors can get to know the city by eating foods like jambalaya. This is made from meat, seafood, vegetables, rice, and spices.

New Orleans is also famous for cakes called beignets. A beignet is like a doughnut without a hole. Beignets are normally eaten for breakfast. However, they are served all day in cafés in an area of the city called the French Quarter. Café du Monde is the most famous of these. It has (**29**). In fact, it only sells beignets and drinks.

People in New Orleans usually drink a kind of coffee called café au lait with their beignets. They use warm milk and a special type of coffee to make this. Long ago, coffee beans were very expensive. People looked for cheaper things that tasted like coffee, and they discovered a plant called chicory. The roots of this plant (**30**) coffee. Over time, the people of New Orleans came to love the taste of coffee made from a mixture of coffee beans and dried chicory roots.

(28) **1** hearing the stories   **2** meeting the people
       3 driving the cars   **4** tasting the dishes

(29) **1** the highest prices   **2** special tables and chairs
       3 a simple menu   **4** only one waiter

(30) **1** contain more vitamins than   **2** have a similar flavor to
       3 grow well in bags of   **4** can be used as cups for

次の英文 [A], [B] の内容に関して，(31) から (37) までの質問に対して最も適切なもの，または文を完成させるのに最も適切なものを 1, 2, 3, 4 の中から一つ選び，その番号を解答用紙の所定欄にマークしなさい。

4

[A]

From: Jenny Smith <jennysmith_060529@ezmail.com>
To: Ai Tanaka <atanaka-1102@tomomail.co.jp>
Date: June 5
Subject: Visit to museum

Hi Ai,

How are things in Japan? I hope that you had fun by the ocean last month. I know how much you love swimming and playing in the sand with your friends. I had a great vacation, too. Last week, I stayed with my aunt and uncle in Pennsylvania. They live on a farm about 50 kilometers from a city called Pittsburgh. My brother and I enjoyed playing outside in nature.

One day, it rained, so we decided to go into the city and see the natural history museum there. The museum was cool because it has many dinosaur bones. It also has an amazing collection of colorful rocks. My favorite part was the "PaleoLab," though. There, scientists prepare old bones from dinosaurs and other animals for the museum. The scientists work in a special room with a large window, so museum visitors can watch them.

My mom says there is a natural history museum here in Chicago, too. She said that she would take you, me, and my brother there when you come to visit the United States next month. We can spend the whole day at the museum if we go early. Let me know if you're interested. I can't wait to see you!

Your pen pal,

Jenny

(31) Last month, Ai

    1 spent some time at a beach.
    2 started taking swimming lessons.
    3 visited her family in Pittsburgh.
    4 played outside with her brother.

(32) What did Jenny like best about the museum?

    1 Watching scientists get bones ready for the museum.
    2 Listening to a cool talk about some dinosaur bones.
    3 Its amazing collection of colorful rocks.
    4 Its windows were large and let in a lot of light.

(33) What is Ai going to do next month?

    1 Move to Chicago with her family.
    2 Take a trip abroad to see Jenny.
    3 Get up early to attend an event.
    4 Start working in a history museum.

[B]
The Return of the Wolves

Wolves are intelligent animals that live in groups called packs. Long ago, packs of wolves could be found in many European countries, including Germany. However, farmers hunted wolves because they sometimes killed the farmers' sheep. Other people hunted wolves for sport. By the 19th century, there were no wolves left in Germany. In the last 20 years, though, wolves have started to return to the country.

In the 1980s and 1990s, European countries made laws to protect wildlife and created special areas for wild animals. At the same time, many people left their farms in eastern Europe to take jobs abroad. The result was that there were fewer people and more safe places for deer and other animals that wolves like to eat. As the number of these animals increased, the number of wolves increased, too. The wolves spread west, and in 2001, they were found living in Germany again.

There are now over 120 packs of wolves in Germany, but not all of them live in the special areas for wild animals. A lot of wolves prefer places that the army uses for training. Experts think this is because these places are safe for the wolves. It seems that some people have been hunting wolves in Germany, even though they are not allowed to. However, these people are afraid of entering army training centers because they might get caught.

Other animals, including rare birds, have also been protected by army training centers. There used to be many army training centers in Europe. However, some of them are no longer needed. In 2015, the German government created parks for wildlife from 62 old army training centers. This increased the total size of such parks in the country by 25 percent. Now, there are plans to bring back horses, bison, and other wild animals to these parks, too.

(34) What is one reason that wolves disappeared from Germany?

    1 They were hunted to stop them from killing farm animals.
    2 The animals that wolves ate were all killed by farmers.
    3 Farmers in Germany started keeping cows instead of sheep.
    4 People made farms in the places where the wolves lived.

(35) Why did many people in eastern Europe leave their farms in the 1980s and 1990s?

    1 Their farms were bought to create areas for wild animals.
    2 The number of wolves and other animals suddenly increased.
    3 New laws in European countries said that they had to leave.
    4 They had chances to go and work in other countries.

(36) Many wolves prefer living in army training centers because

    1 the soldiers at the centers give them food from the kitchens.
    2 people who hunt them are too scared to go in the centers.
    3 a lot of people visit the special areas for wild animals.
    4 there are fewer roads than in other parts of Germany.

(37) The German government

    1 plans to open 62 new army training centers.
    2 moved some rare birds to protect them.
    3 brought horses and bison to parks in 2015.
    4 has provided more land for wild animals.

5
- ●あなたは，外国人の知り合いから以下の **QUESTION** をされました。
- ● **QUESTION** について，あなたの意見とその<u>理由を 2 つ</u>英文で書きなさい。
- ●語数の目安は **50 語～60 語**です。
- ●解答は，解答用紙の **B** 面にあるライティング解答欄に書きなさい。<u>なお，解答欄の外に書かれたものは採点されません。</u>
- ●解答が **QUESTION** に対応していないと判断された場合は，<u>**0** 点と採点されることがあります。</u> **QUESTION** をよく読んでから答えてください。

QUESTION

Do you think it is a good idea for people to learn how to cook by using the Internet?

（リスニングテストは次のページにあります。）

リスニング

準2級リスニングテストについて

1　このリスニングテストには，第1部から第3部まであります。
　　☆英文はすべて一度しか読まれません。
　　第1部：対話を聞き，その最後の文に対する応答として最も適切なものを，放送される
　　　　　1, 2, 3の中から一つ選びなさい。
　　第2部：対話を聞き，その質問に対して最も適切なものを1, 2, 3, 4の中から一つ選
　　　　　びなさい。
　　第3部：英文を聞き，その質問に対して最も適切なものを1, 2, 3, 4の中から一つ選
　　　　　びなさい。
2　No. 30のあと，10秒すると試験終了の合図がありますので，筆記用具を置いてください。

‖‖‖ 第1部 ‖‖‖‖‖‖‖‖‖‖‖‖‖‖‖‖‖‖‖‖‖‖‖‖　◀)) ▶MP3 ▶アプリ ▶CD3 **1**～**11**

No. 1〜No. 10（選択肢はすべて放送されます。）

‖‖‖ 第2部 ‖‖‖‖‖‖‖‖‖‖‖‖‖‖‖‖‖‖‖‖‖‖‖‖　◀)) ▶MP3 ▶アプリ ▶CD3 **12**～**22**

No. 11	1 Write a history report for him.
	2 Visit his sister with him.
	3 Study for the test alone.
	4 Go to a soccer game with him.

No. 12	1 Make a reservation.
	2 Wait in the waiting area.
	3 Order his meal.
	4 Call another restaurant.

No. 13	1 Return his library books.
	2 Work on a report with Carol.
	3 Go to his hockey game.
	4 Record a TV show.

No. 14	1 He had an accident.
	2 He took the wrong bicycle.
	3 He lost his jacket.
	4 He got sick.

No. 15	1 He cannot see the movie he wanted to see.
	2 He could not rent a DVD for his grandson.
	3 *Bubbles the Dancing Bear* was boring.
	4 The Showtime Theater is closing soon.

No. 16	1 By giving him directions to another shop.
	2 By telling him how he can get a discount.
	3 By ordering a copy of *Sporting Life*.
	4 By contacting other stores.

No. 17	1 It is Friday night.
	2 DVDs are on sale.
	3 It has just opened.
	4 A famous singer will be there.

No. 18	1 He does not have any medicine.
	2 He cannot get an appointment.
	3 He has been having headaches.
	4 He has a lot to do this afternoon.

No. 19	1 Buy a doll for her friend.
	2 Look for another gift.
	3 Borrow some money.
	4 Go on a long trip.

No. 20	1 Take money out of the bank.
	2 Look for a green blanket.
	3 Buy the red sofa.
	4 Go to a different store.

No. 21
1 She saw one in a store's magazine.
2 A friend showed her some online.
3 The bookstore near her had one.
4 There was a cheap one at a café.

No. 22
1 Eat leaves instead of small animals.
2 Hide inside tall trees.
3 Make their hearts stop.
4 Move to warmer areas.

No. 23
1 He liked the sound of the engine.
2 He thought the color was great.
3 The height of the front light looked perfect.
4 The salesman gave him a discount.

No. 24
1 Her bus was late again.
2 Her test score was not good.
3 She could not do her homework.
4 She studied for the wrong test.

No. 25
1 A bag has been found near the entrance.
2 New staff members are wanted.
3 Fruit is being sold cheaply.
4 The store will close soon.

No. 26
1 The dog was very young.
2 The dog ran to her.
3 The dog took her ball.
4 The dog was big.

No. 27
1 Meet his friends on Sunday.
2 Start taking jazz lessons.
3 Teach people to play the piano.
4 Perform at a restaurant.

No. 28	1 Aztec children played games with rules.
	2 Aztec women ate much more than men did.
	3 The Aztecs had a kind of chewing gum.
	4 The Aztecs made simple toothbrushes.

No. 29	1 By calling and answering questions.
	2 By hurrying to a stadium's ticket office.
	3 By sending an e-mail to an announcer.
	4 By singing a song by the Boaties.

No. 30	1 Ask his grandparents for a gift.
	2 Buy a new game.
	3 Record a video message.
	4 Make a birthday card.

Tourist Information Centers

There are many tourist information centers around Japan. These centers have a variety of information about local tourist spots. Today, many tourist information centers offer guidebooks in different languages, and in this way they help foreign visitors to find tourist spots easily. These centers will play a more important role in the future.

A

B

Questions

No. 1 According to the passage, how do many tourist information centers help foreign visitors to find tourist spots easily?

No. 2 Now, please look at the people in Picture A. They are doing different things. Tell me as much as you can about what they are doing.

No. 3 Now, look at the woman in Picture B. Please describe the situation.

Now, Mr. / Ms. _____, please turn over the card and put it down.

No. 4 Do you think traveling by train is better than traveling by car?
Yes. → Why?
No. → Why not?

No. 5 Today in Japan, some students study English and another foreign language. Are you interested in studying another foreign language?
Yes. → Please tell me more.
No. → Why not?

Reading Skills

Reading is a very important skill for learning about things. Today, however, some teachers say that students need more help with their reading skills. Many students exchange only short messages on their smartphones, so they sometimes have trouble understanding long passages. Students need to have good reading skills to learn things better.

A

B

Questions

No. 1 According to the passage, why do many students sometimes have trouble understanding long passages?

No. 2 Now, please look at the people in Picture A. They are doing different things. Tell me as much as you can about what they are doing.

No. 3 Now, look at the boy in Picture B. Please describe the situation.

Now, Mr. / Ms. _____, please turn over the card and put it down.

No. 4 Do you think people will spend more money on smartphones in the future?
Yes. → Why?
No. → Why not?

No. 5 These days, many Japanese people have jobs in foreign countries. Would you like to work abroad?
Yes. → Please tell me more.
No. → Why not?

2021-3

一次試験 2022.1.23実施
二次試験 A日程 2022.2.20実施
　　　　 B日程 2022.2.27実施

Grade Pre-2

Pre

試験時間

筆記：75分

リスニング：約25分

＊解答・解説は別冊p.185〜220にあります。
＊面接の流れは本書p.24にあります。

1 次の **(1)** から **(20)** までの (　　) に入れるのに最も適切なものを **1, 2, 3, 4** の中から一つ選び，その番号を解答用紙の所定欄にマークしなさい。

(1) **A:** I finished cleaning my room, Mom. Take a look.
B: It's not good (　　), Kevin. You must clean your desk and put your books away too.
1 enough　　　2 almost　　　3 ahead　　　4 even

(2) **A:** How can I find more (　　) about the cleaning service on your website?
B: Just click on the information button at the top of our home page and you can see everything.
1 rounds　　　2 seasons　　　3 wheels　　　4 details

(3) The United States of America (　　) of 50 states. The smallest state in the country is Rhode Island, and the largest is Alaska.
1 warns　　　2 dreams　　　3 prays　　　4 consists

(4) Recently, the economy has been very good in the western part of the country, so a lot of people have gone there to (　　) jobs.
1 send　　　2 explain　　　3 seek　　　4 mention

(5) Michelle, Sarah, and Roger love to play music, so they have decided to (　　) a band. They will call their new band The Celery Sticks.
1 form　　　2 lift　　　3 sew　　　4 major

(6) Linda keeps (　　) information such as her e-mail and bank passwords in a small notebook. She is careful not to let anyone else see the notebook.
1 impossible　　　2 liquid　　　3 tiring　　　4 secret

(7) Richard broke his leg when he went snowboarding last month. He was absent from school for several days because of his (　　).
1 climate　　　2 injury　　　3 option　　　4 praise

(8) Bart has been looking forward to his grandmother's visit for months. She will come tomorrow, and he is excited about her (   ).

1 arrival   **2** direction   **3** material   **4** connection

(9) *A:* Why were you late for work today, Bob?
B: The (   ) was terrible. It took me an hour to drive 4 kilometers.

1 entrance   **2** image   **3** traffic   **4** fossil

(10) Scott (   ) through his homework so that he could watch his favorite TV show. Because of this, he made many mistakes and did not get many answers right.

1 repeated   **2** tapped   **3** printed   **4** hurried

(11) Mrs. Green decided to give a role to each student in the musical at the school festival. This way, every student could (   ) the performance.

1 play a joke on   **2** play a part in
3 keep track of   **4** keep pace with

(12) *A:* (   ) this website, Leonardo da Vinci was born in 1451.
B: That's not what my textbook says. It says he was born in 1452.

1 Hoping for   **2** Adding up
3 According to   **4** Hiding from

(13) *A:* Have you (   ) Fred recently?
B: Yes. I got a message from him the other day. He said that he's enjoying college.

1 paid for   **2** passed by   **3** heard from   **4** talked over

(14) *A:* What does this word mean, Dad?
B: I'm not sure. You'll have to (   ) in the dictionary.

1 throw it away   **2** take it away
3 save it up   **4** look it up

(15) *A:* Do you know any good sightseeing places in London?
B: Of course! I go there (   ) on business, so I know the city really well.

1 at last   **2** in the end   **3** all the time   **4** for once

(16) Nick is nearly three years old. He always wants to touch the new things he finds every day. He is very curious (   ) anything he hasn't seen before.

1 at   **2** over   **3** about   **4** from

(17) *A:* I made these cookies for everyone this morning. Please (   ) yourself.
B: Thanks. They look delicious.

1 set   **2** take   **3** dress   **4** help

(18) *A:* Dad, this box is too heavy for me (   ) upstairs.
B: OK. I'll take it upstairs for you.

1 to carry   **2** carrying   **3** not carry   **4** be carried

(19) *A:* I have so much homework to do this weekend.
B: So (   ). I have a science report, a history assignment, and an English paper to write for Monday.

1 am I   **2** I am   **3** do I   **4** I do

(20) Hector wants a dog, but his family lives in a small apartment, and there is no space to keep a pet. He wishes he (   ) in a bigger place.

1 lives   **2** to live   **3** is living   **4** lived

次の四つの会話文を完成させるために，(21) から (25) に入るものとして最も適切なものを 1, 2, 3, 4 の中から一つ選び，その番号を解答用紙の所定欄にマークしなさい。

(21) *A:* Hi, Mary. Are you going to come to the movies with us tomorrow?

B: I don't think so. I have some important homework that I need to do first.

A: Why don't you (**21**)?

B: I want to, but my mom asked me to take care of my baby brother.

1 choose an easier topic for it
2 talk to your teacher about it
3 bring it to the movie theater
4 try to finish it this evening

---

(22) *A:* Excuse me. I think I left my scarf on one of your buses.

B: Can you describe what it looks like?

A: Actually, I (**22**).

B: Oh, I see. I think someone brought in a scarf that looks like that. Let me check.

1 have a photo of it on my phone
2 was on the 10:15 bus from Shelby
3 got it as a birthday present
4 had a seat in the back

---

(23) *A:* Mom, can I go to the park to play with my friends?

B: Of course. (**23**).

A: But it's so windy today. It might blow away.

B: I know, but it's really hot outside. Take this one. It has a strap to keep it on your head.

1 Please take a bottle of water
2 You should take your kite
3 Make sure you wear a hat
4 Don't forget your umbrella

A: Thank you for calling Blimpton Animal Hospital. How can I help you?

B: My name is Joan Taylor. I'm calling about my dog, Brownie.

A: What's wrong with Brownie?

B: She hasn't (**24**) for the last two days.

A: I see. Is it the same kind that you usually give her?

B: Yes. She normally loves it. Could (**25**)?

A: Sure. He has time at 11:30 or after 4:00.

B: I have to work this afternoon, so I'll bring Brownie at 11:30.

(24) 1 had much energy
2 been eating her food
3 gotten out of her basket
4 played with her toys

(25) 1 you tell me what the problem is
2 I get some medicine for her
3 the doctor see her today
4 it be a toothache

（筆記試験の問題は次のページに続きます。）

次の英文 [A], [B] を読み，その文意にそって (26) から (30) までの (　　) に入れるのに最も適切なものを 1, 2, 3, 4 の中から一つ選び，その番号を解答用紙の所定欄にマークしなさい。

[A]

Lost for Words

Keiko is 65 years old. She retired from her job a few months ago. When she was working, she was always very busy. She had no time for hobbies. However, she now has plenty of free time. She enjoys gardening, reading books, and going for walks in the countryside. She also (**26**). She really enjoys learning a foreign language and using it to speak with her classmates and her teacher, Mr. Lopez.

One day, Mr. Lopez asked Keiko to talk about her family in class. There were many things that she wanted to say, but she could not say them. She was disappointed because she did not know all the words that she needed. Mr. Lopez tried to (**27**). He said that she is doing really well. If she keeps studying and practicing hard, she will soon find it easy to talk about anything.

(26) **1** takes Spanish lessons　　**2** is a volunteer at a hospital

　　　3 likes to paint pictures　　**4** joined a yoga class

(27) **1** find her textbook　　**2** cheer her up

　　　3 repair her bag　　**4** show her around

[B]

Pest Protection

Insects and other animals often make trouble for farmers. Such animals are known as pests and can be a big problem. They eat the fruits and vegetables that should be sold as food. They also carry diseases to the plants grown on farms. (28) costs farmers a lot of money. Many farmers use chemicals to keep pests away. These chemicals can be bad for the environment, though. They can kill other creatures. They can also get into the fruits and vegetables that people eat.

The owners of the Vergenoegd Low wine farm in South Africa use a different method. They want to stop pests from eating their grapes. At the same time, they do not want any chemicals to get in their wine. Their solution is to (29) to remove pests. Every day, a team of over 1,000 ducks is taken to the fields where the grapes are grown. The ducks spend all day walking around the plants and eating the pests.

Although ducks have been used to control pests in rice fields in Asia for hundreds of years, the use of ducks in other places is much less common. The ducks used on the Vergenoegd Low wine farm are a special kind. They have (30) than other kinds of ducks. As a result, they cannot fly away. Using ducks to control pests also has another advantage. Their waste helps the grape plants to grow.

(28) 1 The weather   2 The damage

3 Buying land   4 Picking fruit

(29) 1 get local children   2 move their plants

3 build tall fences   4 use other animals

(30) 1 more babies each year   2 more colorful bodies

3 much louder voices   4 much shorter wings

4

[A]

From: Joe Hess <joe-hess@kmail.com>
To: Pete Hess <p-hess22@yeehaw.com>
Date: January 23
Subject: Ontario trip

Hi Pete,

Are you excited about our trip to Ontario next month? I bought my ticket to Ontario and my return ticket yesterday. My plane leaves Chicago at 11 a.m. on February 8. The flight takes only one and a half hours. Have you bought your tickets yet? What time will you leave New York City?

Anyway, do you remember what we talked about on the phone last week? You said that you want to go fishing during our trip. My neighbor goes on fishing trips in Ontario every fall. She told me about a company that offers one-day fishing tours of Lake Huron. The company's name is Great Fish, and it costs $300 for two people. The tour will start at 8 a.m. and finish at 4 p.m., and the price includes lunch.

I'll call the company tonight and make a reservation for February 10. My neighbor also said that we need special licenses to fish in Ontario. We can get them online, or we can buy them at a sports shop in Ontario. I think we should buy them on the Internet before we go. A one-day license costs about $20. I can't wait to go!

Your brother,
Joe

(31) What will Joe do in February?

    1 Buy plane tickets to Chicago.
    2 Go on vacation with Pete.
    3 Visit New York City.
    4 Move to a new home in Ontario.

(32) Joe's neighbor

    1 gave Joe a tour of Lake Huron.
    2 said Joe could use her fishing boat.
    3 told Joe about a fishing tour company.
    4 recommended a restaurant to Joe.

(33) How does Joe suggest he and Pete get licenses?

    1 By going to a sports shop to get them.
    2 By buying them from a website.
    3 By ordering them on the phone.
    4 By asking a company to reserve them.

[B]
The Mystery of the Crannogs

In some lakes in Scotland and Ireland, there are small man-made islands. These are called crannogs, and they were built long ago with large rocks that were carried into the lakes. Building the crannogs was probably a lot of hard work because some of the rocks weigh 250 kilograms. What is more, the crannogs are between 10 and 30 meters wide and connected to the land by a bridge made of rocks. Although there are over a thousand of them, no one knows the reason why they were made.

Experts used to think that the crannogs were built about 3,000 years ago. However, a recent discovery shows that some of the crannogs are much older. A diver found some broken pots in the water around the crannogs in a lake on the island of Lewis. Scientists discovered that the pots were over 5,000 years old. This led to further research and the discovery of similar items in other lakes with crannogs.

The pots were in good condition, and it was clear to researchers that they had not been used much before they were dropped in the lakes. The researchers believe that the pots were probably used for special ceremonies on the crannogs. It is not clear what the purpose of the ceremonies was, though, because there are no written records from the time when they were held.

Two thousand years after the oldest crannogs were built, people began living on them. This is shown by old pieces of wood from their houses that have been found on the crannogs. When these people built their houses, they probably damaged the crannogs. This made it difficult to find out why the crannogs were built. Researchers are continuing to look for things to solve the mystery of the crannogs, but it may take many years for them to do so.

(34) Crannogs are

    1 man-made lakes in Scotland and Ireland.
    2 islands made by people a long time ago.
    3 walls built with large rocks.
    4 bridges that were built across lakes.

(35) The discovery of some broken pots has

    1 allowed people to find out how the crannogs were built.
    2 proved that there are more crannogs than scientists thought.
    3 changed experts' ideas about how old some crannogs are.
    4 shown that it may be too dangerous to dive in these lakes.

(36) What do researchers think that the pots that they found were used for?

    1 For decorating people's homes.
    2 For important events.
    3 To keep written records.
    4 To catch fish in the lakes.

(37) Why is it difficult to know the reason that the crannogs were made?

    1 Researchers think they lost some things that they found on them.
    2 People may have damaged them when they built their homes.
    3 Old pieces of wood might have been removed from them.
    4 The people who made them probably moved away long ago.

5
●あなたは，外国人の知り合いから以下の **QUESTION** をされました。

● **QUESTION** について，あなたの意見とその理由を 2 つ英文で書きなさい。

●語数の目安は **50 語～60 語**です。

●解答は，解答用紙の **B** 面にあるライティング解答欄に書きなさい。なお，解答欄の外に書かれたものは採点されません。

●解答が **QUESTION** に対応していないと判断された場合は，0 点と採点されることがあります。 **QUESTION** をよく読んでから答えてください。

QUESTION

Do you think there should be more sports programs on TV?

（リスニングテストは次のページにあります。）

リスニング

準2級リスニングテストについて

1 このリスニングテストには，第1部から第3部まであります。
☆英文はすべて一度しか読まれません。
第1部：対話を聞き，その最後の文に対する応答として最も適切なものを，放送される1，2，3の中から一つ選びなさい。
第2部：対話を聞き，その質問に対して最も適切なものを1，2，3，4の中から一つ選びなさい。
第3部：英文を聞き，その質問に対して最も適切なものを1，2，3，4の中から一つ選びなさい。

2 No. 30 のあと，10秒すると試験終了の合図がありますので，筆記用具を置いてください。

第1部 ◀» ▶MP3 ▶アプリ ▶CD 3 43～53

No. 1～No. 10（選択肢はすべて放送されます。）

第2部 ◀» ▶MP3 ▶アプリ ▶CD 3 54～64

No. 11	1 They are all sold out.
	2 He called the wrong restaurant.
	3 There is a mistake on the menu.
	4 His house is too far for deliveries.

No. 12	1 Borrow some books.
	2 Study at a friend's house.
	3 Go to a concert.
	4 Buy some tickets.

No. 13	1 The waiter is too busy to help her.
	2 The waiter brought her the wrong food.
	3 She did not order dessert.
	4 She does not like apple pie.

No. 14
1 By delivering it herself.
2 By regular mail.
3 By overnight delivery.
4 By bicycle delivery.

No. 15
1 Get a present for a child.
2 Make clothes for her family.
3 Take pictures of her baby.
4 Play with her friend's children.

No. 16
1 She wants him to fix her coat.
2 She wants him to buy a new button.
3 He did not give her a refund.
4 He did not damage her coat button.

No. 17
1 Make a salad for the woman.
2 Eat both kinds of pizza.
3 Order salad and pizza.
4 Change his order from salad to pizza.

No. 18
1 Take her son to a baseball game.
2 Look for her son's baseball glove.
3 Finish her e-mail.
4 Help move a desk.

No. 19
1 Her hair may get wet.
2 Her husband is sick.
3 The party may be canceled.
4 The bus is late.

No. 20
1 Call their hotel.
2 Wait for the next train.
3 Get cash from an ATM.
4 Talk to a taxi driver.

No. 21
1 Buy a cake for his grandfather.
2 Give his grandmother some flowers.
3 Work at his grandparents' store.
4 Help his grandmother in the garden.

No. 22
1 They used popular black paper.
2 They used the same symbols as modern cards.
3 They were considered to be luxury items.
4 They were made to study history.

No. 23
1 Her school does not have a band club.
2 It is difficult to learn an instrument.
3 The band members played very well.
4 The concert was not so long.

No. 24
1 There may be delays later in the day.
2 A hockey game has been canceled.
3 Trains are currently stopped.
4 Passengers should get off at the next station.

No. 25
1 She will go to a bicycle store.
2 She will play video games.
3 She will go to a birthday party.
4 She will ride her bicycle.

No. 26
1 He has not been to Hawaii.
2 He cannot find his passport.
3 He arrives in two hours.
4 He has lost his bag and coat.

No. 27
1 They make people's tongues sweat.
2 They taste differently on very hot days.
3 They are used in food to keep it hot.
4 They create a feeling of pain.

No. 28	1 He got a new chess set.
	2 He learned how to play chess.
	3 He played in a chess competition.
	4 He joined a chess club.

No. 29	1 An expert will talk about sharks.
	2 An artist will draw pictures of the ocean.
	3 The announcer will dress up as a shark.
	4 The viewers will discuss ocean swimming.

No. 30	1 He will stay at home.
	2 He will visit his family.
	3 He will study at college.
	4 He will go on a trip.

問題カード（A日程）　　◀)) ▶MP3 ▶アプリ ▶CD 3 76〜80

Passwords

People sometimes need passwords when using the Internet. However, using the same password for a long time can be dangerous. Now, many websites ask people to change passwords more often, and by doing so they help people protect personal information. It is important that people keep strangers from seeing their personal information.

A

B

Questions

No. 1 According to the passage, how do many websites help people protect personal information?

No. 2 Now, please look at the people in Picture A. They are doing different things. Tell me as much as you can about what they are doing.

No. 3 Now, look at the woman in Picture B. Please describe the situation.

Now, Mr. / Ms. _____, please turn over the card and put it down.

No. 4 Do you think it is good for children to use the Internet?
Yes. → Why?
No. → Why not?

No. 5 Many people enjoy doing outdoor activities in winter. Do you do any outdoor activities in winter?
Yes. → Please tell me more.
No. → Why not?

Festivals in Japan

There are many kinds of festivals in Japan. Large cities, small towns, and villages usually have their own festivals. Many of these festivals are held in summer or fall. Japanese festivals often show traditional culture to visitors, so they are popular with foreign tourists. Festivals are attracting more and more attention.

A

B

Questions

No. 1   According to the passage, why are Japanese festivals popular with foreign tourists?

No. 2   Now, please look at the people in Picture A. They are doing different things. Tell me as much as you can about what they are doing.

No. 3   Now, look at the man and the woman in Picture B. Please describe the situation.

Now, Mr. / Ms. _____, please turn over the card and put it down.

No. 4   Do you think towns and cities in Japan should have more libraries?
Yes. → Why?
No. → Why not?

No. 5   Today, many people are careful about their health. Do you do anything for your health?
Yes. → Please tell me more.
No. → Why not?

旺文社の英検®書

☆ **一発合格したいなら「全問＋パス単」！**

旺文社が自信を持っておすすめする王道の組み合わせです。

☆ 過去問で出題傾向をしっかりつかむ！
英検®過去6回全問題集 1～5級
音声アプリ対応　音声ダウンロード　別売CDあり

☆ 過去問を徹底分析した「でる順」！
英検®でる順パス単 1～5級
音声アプリ対応　音声ダウンロード

模試　本番形式の予想問題で総仕上げ！
7日間完成 英検®予想問題ドリル 1～5級
CD付　音声アプリ対応

参考書　申し込みから面接まで英検のすべてがわかる！
英検®総合対策教本 1～5級
CD付

問題集　大問ごとに一次試験を集中攻略！
DAILY英検®集中ゼミ 1～5級
音声アプリ対応　音声ダウンロード

二次対策　動画で面接をリアルに体験！
英検®二次試験・面接完全予想問題 1～3級
DVD＋CD付　音声アプリ対応

このほかにも多数のラインナップを揃えております。

 旺文社の英検®合格ナビゲーター
https://eiken.obunsha.co.jp/
英検合格を目指す方のためのウェブサイト。
試験情報や級別学習法, おすすめの英検書を紹介しています。

※英検®は、公益財団法人 日本英語検定協会の登録商標です。

株式会社 旺文社　〒162-8680 東京都新宿区横寺町55
https://www.obunsha.co.jp/

 Obunsha

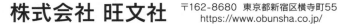